T0354795

OUR TIME IS NOW

A Woman's Guide to Creating a Life and World You Will Love

Mary Ann Daly, M.A.

BALBOA.
PRESS
A DIVISION OF HAY HOUSE

Balboa Press books may be ordered through booksellers or by contacting:

Balboa Press
A Division of Hay House
1663 Liberty Drive
Bloomington, IN 47403
www.balboapress.com
1 (877) 407-4847

Because of the dynamic nature of the Internet, any web addresses or links contained in this book may have changed since publication and may no longer be valid. The views expressed in this work are solely those of the author and do not necessarily reflect the views of the publisher, and the publisher hereby disclaims any responsibility for them.

The author of this book does not dispense medical advice or prescribe the use of any technique as a form of treatment for physical, emotional, or medical problems without the advice of a physician, either directly or indirectly. The intent of the author is only to offer information of a general nature to help you in your quest for emotional and spiritual well-being. In the event you use any of the information in this book for yourself, which is your constitutional right, the author and the publisher assume no responsibility for your actions.

Any people depicted in stock imagery provided by Thinkstock are models, and such images are being used for illustrative purposes only.
Certain stock imagery © Thinkstock.

Print information available on the last page.

ISBN: 978-1-5043-2932-3 (sc)
ISBN: 978-1-5043-2934-7 (hc)
ISBN: 978-1-5043-2933-0 (e)

Library of Congress Control Number: 2015903661

Balboa Press rev. date: 06/09/2015

Dedicated with much love
and great appreciation to my parents,
Dick and Norine Daly

"The world will be saved by the Western woman."

- His Holiness the Dalai Lama, at the
Vancouver Peace Summit in 2009

Contents

Preface

I always knew I wanted to be a psychotherapist. I just didn't think I could ever go to college, never mind graduate school. But I always knew that being a therapist was my calling. As I share in *OUR TIME IS NOW*, when something is right, things fall into place… and somehow it all fell into place for me to do the work I've now been doing for over 27 years.

Recently, I moved into a new office space. As I prepared to move, I looked through boxes of client files I hadn't seen in years. It was a trip down memory lane filled with the faces and names of some of the best people I've ever met. I smiled throughout. To say it has been an honor and a privilege to work with my clients is an understatement. I can't even begin to describe the depth of love, appreciation and awe that I have for them. I feel teary-eyed just writing this.

To the people who inspired this book—my clients—know that you have all touched my heart in your own special way and I am so blessed that you allowed me to be your guide for part of your life's journey. Know that I am forever grateful for all you have taught me. I wish you a life filled with much joy, laughter and more love than your heart could ever hold.

Peace and blessings,
Mary Ann

Acknowledgements

I've often been surprised by the length of the acknowledgements section in some of my favorite books. After writing OUR TIME IS NOW, I have first-hand knowledge of the reason why. How can I begin to thank the numerous wonderful people who were there for me throughout this journey?

First and foremost, I want to thank my brother Joe. If it wasn't for all the love, help and support you've given me from start to finish, I would never have been able to do this. Words cannot express my appreciation to you. You are an extraordinary husband, father, son, brother and friend, and I am blessed to be your sister and your friend.

The other person who made this book really become a reality is my brother John. John and my beautiful niece Bridget painstakingly helped me go over it piece-by-piece, word-by-word, to ensure smooth organization and flow. I could never have finished this without your assistance. Thank you for offering your help and giving up beautiful summer weekends to work with me when you saw that I was floundering.

Thank you as well to Barb and Caitlin for your input and always-enthusiastic support. It was a pleasure to spend so much time with your wonderful family in your beautiful home. I love all of you.

To Jack Kennedy: You graciously lent me your beautiful lake house time and time again, and provided me with a peaceful and inspiring place to write. Thank you, my friend. You truly are one of the most generous people I know.

To Kat Beaulieu, my closest friend since we were 15 years old. You have always been one of the biggest champions throughout my life and this time is no different. Your love and encouragement have been constant and steadfast, and helped me hang in there whenever I was going through a rough spot. To say I appreciate you is an understatement. You are an incredible woman and I am so blessed that we are friends.

To my big wonderful family: It is with a heart overflowing with love that I thank you for all the encouragement and support you've shown me these years I've been writing. In particular, I want to thank my sister Nancy, who, despite an incredible busy life being a terrific wife to my fabulous brother-in-law LB, raising four wonderful children and running a business, always took time to show interest in my book. You are one of the best moms I've ever known and an amazing businesswoman as well. I am honored to be your sister.

I can't say enough about the help my brother Rick gave me when he offered to read my manuscript in all its rawness. Your feedback was invaluable and helped shape OUR TIME IS NOW into a much better book. You have one of the best hearts of anyone I know and you are one of the best men I've had the privilege to know. How grateful I am to be your sister. As well, a big hug of gratitude goes to my sister-in-law Mary for all the encouragement you've given me throughout this process. And a many thanks to my sister Maggie for your assistance with the copy write. You're the best!

There are several people I want to thank for their willingness and generosity in taking time to read my book drafts. These include Gale Dreas, Elaine Burgher and Gloria Schmorr. Thanks to all of you for your valuable therapist's eye views, insight and feedback. You have my highest regard and respect as professional colleagues, and I treasure our friendships.

My friend Betsy Fallon is one of the first people I shared my writing with. Betsy, you are one of the smartest and most heart-centered businesswomen I've ever known. I truly believe that if there were more women like you running things in business, the world would be a much better place. I can't thank you enough for all of your encouragement and your steadfast support.

To my friend Alyce Sorokie: Thank you so much for being an inspiration. Sharing your journey as an author helped motivate me more than you can know. I also appreciate your consistent interest in what I was writing and the discussions we enjoyed as a result. Talking with you about OUR TIME IS NOW was always thought-provoking and I can't tell you how much it helped me with my writing. I am very grateful to have you in my life.

To my friend and acupuncturist extraordinaire Julie Gaudet: Barnes & Noble lost a great bookstore manager, but the world gained a great acupuncturist when you decided to return to school. Luckily for me, I've benefitted from both of your interests. Thanks for helping me understand the world of books and publishing. And thanks for the extraordinary acupuncture I've received from you which has, I believe, enabled me to be flu-free for the last several years. I really appreciate all the help you give me.

To Sharon Sechrest, to whom I am indebted to for helping me finally come up with a sub-title for this book. Everyone should be so lucky to have a friend like you. You are one of those people that I can just pick up with no matter how long it's been since we've talked. You are a woman of substance and integrity, with a huge heart to boot! You consistently make me think about things in new ways. I have always been grateful to know you.

Right now the word *thanks* seems so inadequate, but it is with great thanks and appreciation that I acknowledge the following friends for their time, listening, sharing, encouragement, enthusiasm and support: June Simonian, Sharon Guffrai, MaryBeth Hughes, Pat Lauer Bertsche, Roneen Blank, Marijo Kelly, Patty Strachota, Annie Boston Praught DiVirgilio, Steve Parker, Ruthie Rankin, Terry and Carol Herbstritt, Brian Murphy, Anne Coogan, Terri Tuohy, Elizabeth Ward, Analiese Parchen, Julie Murphy Casserly, MaryJo Bowman, Tom Brennan, Tim Gibbons, Candy Frankovelgia, Leslie Marino, Mary Kloepfer, Mary Rose Hamming, Noriene Philbin, and last but by no means least Serita Winthrop. The love and encouragement you all continually bestow upon me is an amazing gift. I have no words for how meaningful your friendships are to me. So suffice it to say, *grazie!*

There are those people in our lives who inspire us and mentor us in ways they may not even realize. I have been incredibly blessed to have several teachers and mentors over the years who helped me become not only a better professional but to grow personally. The first person I want to thank is my college advisor Walt Keller: You sought me out and gave me a hug and kick in the butt at the same time when I really, really needed it. Without your influence, guidance and support I can't even imagine where I might have ended up—but I highly doubt it would have been graduate school. Walt, thank you for being the first person to tell me I was smart.

To Penny Jameson, my undergraduate psychology professor: I am enormously grateful to you. You were a great role model for me. I admired you and learned to work hard because you inspired me to do so. You showed up for me at a critical juncture in my life and gave me invaluable support. There is no way I would've gotten into graduate school without your letter of recommendation. Thank you so much.

To Joan Klagsbrun: My heart always softens when I think of you. You are truly my mentor. How lucky I was to have you as my graduate school advisor! You are an amazing therapist, teacher and woman. Your family therapy course impacted me more than you could ever realize. From the beginning you were there for me, guiding and encouraging me in your kind and inspiring way. I've always admired you, and as a student, wanting to make you proud was great motivation to work harder. I will always have the utmost respect and appreciation for you.

To Jane Gerber, my Chicago mentor: I smile whenever I think of you. You have an amazing life force and are one of the most beloved people I know. You are funny, smart and wise—an incredible and powerful combination. I am so glad I met you. I've learned so much from you that to say thanks seems so inadequate.

To Rich Lessor: You are a wizard. I have met many teachers in my life but few as brilliant as you. Thank you for the consulting work we did together. I value all of what you taught me. You helped make me the therapist that I am.

To Philip Dawson, a very talented playwright and the first person to help me learn about writing: Thank you so much for all of your support. You were a tremendous help in assisting me in getting things off the ground. I'm thrilled for all the success you've attained since we met!

To Jenni Prokopy: How glad I am to have met you in our public speaking class. You've been the one to bring this baby home! You helped organize things in a proficient manner and at the same time kept my voice as you edited. I really appreciate all your hard work and encouragement.

To Mary Beth Hughes and Jim Courtwright of *Big Thinking by the Hour*: You have been with me from the very beginning. Your encouragement has been steady throughout, and you have helped organize things all along the way. You are a great team, very creative, talented and caring. All I can say is thanks for everything.

To Doug Wilke: You created a beautiful piece of art for me and it is more beautiful than I could've imagined. Thank you for you generosity. You have my deepest gratitude and appreciation.

On the back cover are recommendations from two accomplished bestselling authors, Karol Jackowski and Adri Trigiani. In the midst of very busy lives, you each took the time to read OUR TIME IS NOW And I so appreciate the generosity of your enthusiastic and thoughtful endorsements. Kare, I think of you every Ash Wednesday and am so happy we've managed to stay connected all these years. You have been a great role model to me and are one of the most extraordinary and fun people I've ever known. Need I say more. Adri, your books have touched the hearts of everyone who's read them and as you well know, you have many many fans. How many authors literally have fan clubs all over the country! Thank you for your kind words. I look forward to your next book!

Introduction

Ladies, it's OUR time! It's not only our time, but also our *responsibility* to change the world and make it a better place. It's been a "man's world" for most of civilization. And it still is. They've had their chance, and most men and women would agree that at this time in history, things are a mess—a hot mess!

Our time is now. We are needed and we are ready. The women's movement of the 70s precipitated over 40 years of hard-earned opportunities. The choices, possibilities and power that were previously unavailable for most women are now much more acceptable for the majority of contemporary females. Despite this progress, not only men but, sadly, women still often ignore, overlook or minimize one of the most valuable contributions we innately bring to the table. It's what I call Our Feminine Heart Energy.

I believe that in order to make the progress we've made over the last 40 years, we have had to learn the masculine model of power that opens the doors of opportunity. Women during the 70s and 80s who penetrated the traditional male work force even dressed in business suits that replicated what powerful men were wearing. That patriarchal model of power is something we don't need to emulate any more. We know it, we get it, and we are ready to step up to the plate and take our place in the major leagues.

There's an old saying, "take what you need and leave the rest." Now is our time to take the experience and the skills we've learned from the traditional masculine model of power, leave what doesn't work behind and move forward to integrate it with our innate wisdom as women.

Our female biology is an extraordinary gift that connects us to the core wisdom of our hearts. How powerful this is! When we don't take on the old, outdated masculine model of power, this wisdom is indispensable.

Feminine Heart Energy is the essence of how we naturally assume our various roles in life.

It is time for us to collectively become conscious and deliberate in our awareness, appreciation, and use of this gift.

Together, women can (and need) to consciously identify, own and utilize our inner wisdom as a way to contribute to the well-being of the world.

This is the reason for this book. The ultimate purpose of OUR TIME IS NOW is to help YOU to consciously identify, own and utilize your heart energy power, and look at how to integrate it with your skills, tools, education, experience, vision, hopes and dreams. This will not only help further your own personal evolution, but as a result, will organically contribute to those around you and, therefore, the world.

A note about the tools in this book: After each chapter, I offer reflections to help you apply the concepts you are studying. I strongly recommend that you write out your answers, as the act of writing accesses the unconscious part of our brain, and these questions are about getting conscious!

SECTION 1

Identifying

Chapter 1

The Place God Calls You

The Power of Female Relationships

It was my first week at my first job out of graduate school. I was sitting in my first therapy group with eight female clients who were all alcoholics or drug addicts (or both). The first woman to speak that night told me she wanted to rip off my face, and informed me that I looked too healthy and all-American for her taste, then asked what the hell did I know and how the hell could I help her or any of the women there since I wasn't chemically dependent myself. (This is actually the PG version of her comments.)

To say I was intimidated is an understatement. It was baptism by fire as I took on my new role as a counselor at a program for alcoholic and drug-addicted women. It was the beginning of some of the hardest and best work I've accomplished so far.

Even though I had sisters growing up, we were so far apart in age I didn't feel a sisterly connection. When I went to an all-girls high school and subsequently college, I discovered something very special in the sisterhood of women.

My new job only reinforced this. What I began to witness among these women who had been beaten down by the ravages of addiction and histories of trauma was the healing that came from the community of women. This was a tough and sometimes-hardened group of clients. Most of them had major trust issues. And many of these women didn't like other women.

But what I observed was that once they could get past their initial defenses and settle into the feminine presence of one another, the healing

1

really started. They began to open their hearts. This is the power of what I refer to as Feminine Heart Energy. It is the energy that, when tapped into, can create the miracle of recovery. It is the energetic bond and connection that helps facilitate transformation. When utilized in a collective way this Feminine Heart Energy is what can also change the world.

Feminine Heart Energy

What exactly is Feminine Heart Energy? Here's how I've come to know it:

For years in my meditations I've often had visions of my heart as the center of my being. It's been during these times of quiet and reflection I've come to believe that our soul lives in our hearts, and this is why love is such a powerful force.

Our circulatory system carries our blood from our physical hearts throughout the body. Now imagine a similar system—this one invisible—that carries energy from our invisible soul throughout our bodies as well. This energy emanates from the soul, through our hearts, through our arms, and into our hands. That is why the healing power of touch is so strong; our hands are the work organs of our hearts and souls.

If our heart is the home for our soul, then imagine what it means for us to connect more fully with our hearts, both literally and figuratively. It is my belief that the flow of energy from our hearts and souls throughout our bodies is actually the essence of who we are. This is what I call Feminine Heart Energy.

The heart is a collective representation of feminine characteristics. This means it is symbolic of the internal: the collaborative, receptive, nurturing and loving parts of our beings. Similarly, masculine characteristics are symbolized by the external: the competitive, assertive, strong and pragmatic parts of us.

Both women and men have feminine and masculine characteristics, some more than others. I believe the key to health and success is having a balance between both. For too long, however, our world has been ruled by mostly male energy. This imbalance is the source of many of the challenges we face. It is time to incorporate our Feminine Heart Energy with the masculine.

Feminine Heart Energy is About Connecting with the Feminine Life Force More Fully

I believe that women have an easier ability to connect with our feminine life force more fully, as a result of our innate makeup. A purposeful transition of thought and comprehension regarding our heart energy is necessary to develop a new generation of power. I believe that by identifying, owning and utilizing this Feminine Heart Energy, we are capable of fixing the ills of our world and creating a healthier planet. This is how we will restructure our approach to the leadership required to produce the progress necessary for our world's betterment.

I've had the privilege of knowing many extraordinary women: family, friends, teachers, healers, clients, colleagues and more. This book has been birthed by the inspiration, encouragement and strength these women have selflessly given to me. I know I am not alone. I suspect you could say the same thing about the incredible women you've known throughout your life.

As a psychotherapist in private practice for over 25 years, I have often reflected on the numerous women clients I have had the honor of working with, women who have had the courage to do the work necessary to recover from a myriad of problems. These women have histories of depression and anxiety; tragic personal losses; life-threatening illnesses; divorce; addictions; dysfunctional families with generations of incest, violence and chemical dependency; mental illness; sexual and physical assault; and emotional despair. These are amazing women who, as a result of their hard work, have been—and are now—positively impacting our planet in many ways.

I wonder, however: Have these women truly realized their potential? Have all women, in general, realized their full potential? Do women really "get" that they are invaluable contributors, and have the important skills, insights and experiences that are essential to transforming the world?

So I pose this question: What if women—especially the many of you who have been through your own personal growth journey—intentionally used their wisdom, experience, talents, strengths and hope to help transform the world? If so, what would humanity look like?

An Outmoded Model of Power

Much too often we downplay our power or don't identify it as such, because it does not fit the traditional model of power: a male-based model.

A traditionally masculine version of power is about aggression, linear thinking, and competition, rather than collaboration. It is often focused on short-term gain, which creates greed, a "he who has the most toys wins" mentality, and a disregarding attitude toward the value of feelings. The focus is continually on the "bottom line." This type of thinking has very often been dismissive toward women, placing little value on our roles in the home and the world.

This is *not* a criticism of men. I love men; I am simply defining an outmoded model that hasn't worked well for quite some time now.

As women, we understand and know the importance of relationships in a very deep way, in every cell of our being. We don't have to wait until we are dying to comprehend the most important thing in life: Have we loved and been loved enough?

Author Raymond Carver put this so wisely. "…And did you get what you wanted from this life, even so? I did. And what did you want? To call myself *beloved*, to feel myself *beloved* on the earth."

Fortunately, these days, more men than ever are able to connect with their feelings and hearts, to understand the importance of relationship, collaboration and long-term thinking—men who value and respect the wisdom of women. Men who comprehend that greed is NOT good. To me, these evolved men, many of whom were raised purposefully and intentionally to be this way by evolved women, are prime indicators that we are now ready for a feminine model of power.

Women have the inner resources to create an advanced and consciously evolved new breed of power. It is imperative that we take responsibility to do so now. We are at a critical juncture in the timeline of human history. There is tremendous need to create healthier, more functional ways to address the needs and challenges that face our communities, our country and our world.

Unfortunately, for many people, it is not until we are very ill, dying or in some other serious crisis that we are really able to see with our hearts and gain the wisdom to understand what is most important in life: Love. Rather than wait for things to get worse, we women need to intervene *now* to cure that which ails our world. It is crucial for the healing of ourselves and our world that we not wait any longer.

The Place God Calls You

There is a wonderful quote by Frederick Buechner that I keep on my bulletin board: "The place God calls you is the place where your deep gladness and the world's deep hunger meet." This profoundly resonates with me while I write this book and imagine women as leaders and healers working to meet the needs of our world.

As women, our deep gladness usually comes from the relationships in our lives. *It is our feminine nature that moves us to connect with others,* whether as a wife, parent, daughter, sister, friend, neighbor or co-worker. As women, we tend to deeply and innately know, understand and value the power of our relationships.

Our world right now deeply and urgently needs us to focus on what is really important in life, and get into "right" relationships with ourselves and everything around us. This means that our behavior lines up with our values. Right relationships means intentional living; achieving healthy and balanced relationships with our bodies, sex, money, jobs, the economy, home, family, friends, our health, the earth, our neighbors (including our global neighbors), our spiritual beliefs, faith, our community, our country… the list is endless. All the items I've listed have one thing in common: relationships.

Since most women experience relationships as the source of deep gladness in their lives, it seems only natural that women are being called to meet the world's deep needs. It is with this consciousness that you will utilize a new and advanced generation of power to help you gain awareness of how to harness the energy of your body, mind and spirit.

Through this upgraded and revolutionary vision of empowerment we will be discussing in the coming chapters, you will be able to create the relationships, life and world you desire and deserve. The key to the evolution of our well-being—and that of families, society and the world—is inside of us. It is about tapping into a healthier, regenerative source of power by valuing ourselves as women, and seeing clearly how our Feminine Heart Energy is the critical essence to create global survival and growth.

Reflections:

1. Imagine what a "woman's world" would look like. What would be different?
2. Do you know where the place is that God calls you?
3. Who or what is it that makes your heart sing and how might this be related to the above question?
4. In what areas of your life are you in "right relationship" with yourself? What areas you are not in "right relationship" with yourself?

Chapter 2

Nature vs. Nurture

Knowing how to develop and maintain relationships is at the heart of success. This is true in marriage, business, politics, education, religion and even healthcare. *As women, we understand the importance of relationships in every cell of our beings.* Is this nature or nurture? I believe it's both. As I said previously, I think woman have an innate ability to value relationships, and I also think this ability is encouraged and nurtured by families and society in general.

In college I read two research studies that showed the differences between boys and girls. Since I went to college over 35 years ago, I am unfortunately unable to cite the origin of these studies. However, I was obviously struck by them as I still remember them after all these years.

In one study, the researchers observed four-year-old children's play rituals. They noted that the girls were far more invested in the relationships between each other than in the game itself. During the course of play, when someone's feelings got hurt, the girls consistently adapted the rules to accommodate one another.

What the researchers observed in the boys was quite the opposite: the boys were far more involved in the task aspect of play. For example, if one of the boys didn't like something, rather than attempt to change the rules, he would quit the game. The rules were the critical piece for the boys; relationships were much less crucial in their play.

The other study observed preschoolers going to birthday parties. This study found that girls were typically invited by their mothers to be very involved in the entire gift giving process. The mothers would take the girls shopping and ask for their input on the choice of gift, cards, wrapping and party outfits. Throughout this process, mother and daughter were often observed talking excitedly about the upcoming party.

In contrast, the boys were much less involved. Most often they'd be told what to wear, handed a wrapped gift, reminded to behave and told when they would be picked up. Quite a difference! Based on this study it's understandable why women are often confused and upset when men don't put much thought into gift giving and why men "don't get" why it's so important to many women.

In the first study, the children were left to their own devices, and in the second, they were guided by their mothers. Obviously many of the differences between boys and girls are learned, but I am also convinced that a great deal of those differences are innate.

The problem, as I see it, is that when men don't operate the way women do; we tend to take it personally. I challenge you to "get" that the critical issue for us at this time is to value, appreciate, celebrate and respect ourselves and the important ways we are different from men! When we get frustrated with men for not having our innate gifts, we give our power away.

If you really stop and think about it, we are looking for men to be like us in order to validate ourselves. Our job at this point is for us to "get it" when it comes to how amazing we are because we are women!

There's a saying in 12 Step programs: "You spot it, you got it." This means that when we react strongly in a negative way to someone, it is usually because unconsciously, they are reflecting back to us a part of ourselves that we do not like. Anyone who has ever walked through the door of a therapist's office should be familiar with this concept.

The therapeutic process usually requires us to look at ourselves in this way in order help us become more conscious. This is a valuable tool to assist us in taking responsibility for our feelings and behavior. When we are able see how we are "hooked" by someone else's behaviors or attitudes from this new perspective, it usually dispels the negativity towards that other person. Energetically, there is a shift; we no longer feel "hooked," and they no longer have power over us.

Let's take a look at the things that tend to bother women about men, and keep in mind that perhaps these are things that reflect an unappealing part of ourselves. For example, how often do women complain that men just "don't get it?" Keep in mind that perhaps these are things that reflect an unappealing part of ourselves. The following story is a demonstration of how we often just "don't get it" ourselves!

Susan's Story: A New Way of Seeing

Susan is an immediately likable woman. She is bright, fun, talented, a successful business woman and a caring and involved mom. She is very skilled at expressing and communicating her needs.

I had seen Susan previously for therapy, and after she completed her course of treatment, she would come see me from time to time for "tune-ups." So when Susan walked into my office, agitatedly plopped herself on my couch and began venting, I listened closely.

She was angry and frustrated with her husband… again. Same old, same old. She told me how sick and tired she was of having to be the one who raised the important issues in their relationship. They'd been out of sync for several weeks, and he seemed not to notice. She described being the one who always had to initiate talking about what was going on between them. She was angry about this being her job in the relationship.

Sound familiar, ladies? She shared her frustration that this extra responsibility had become an even bigger problem than the issues she'd brought to him in the first place. She finished spewing and sat back, frustrated, looking at me in a conspiratorial manner, certain (I'm sure) that as another woman I would "get it" about how "men don't get it."

Boy, was she in for a surprise. And quite frankly, so was I, as I blurted out the words "get over it." Yes I really did say those words! I was as shocked at myself as she was, by the look on her face.

Normally, my training and experience would lead me to assist Susan in looking at how she could take responsibility to "communicate her needs" to her husband. We might even practice helpful ways to do so. On this day, however, a light bulb went off for me. I was able to see her and this all-too-common struggle between men and women (myself included) from a wonderful new perspective!

That day, I saw her with fresh eyes. I saw her as a woman who has an incredible skill, one far easier for most women to access than most men.

This skill is the ability to identify and communicate feelings, to "know" when something's right or not.

Susan was unaware that what she was really complaining about was her own special ability to contribute something loving and beautiful to her marriage. From this perspective neither she, nor her husband, are wrong. It just means that she has the capacity to shine a light on issues that need to be addressed in order to have a healthy marriage.

I challenged Susan to take another look at her situation. I invited her to begin to see that her husband—a good man—had no clue how to do what she had done innately. We discussed how her built-in radar (her feminine awareness of when things are off-track between them) was a gift she brought to their relationship.

This intrinsic "knowing" was an emotional navigational system for the well-being of their marriage. Susan needed to "get" that she was the one who was blessed to come into the world with this custom feature already included!

Having A New Perspective is Experiencing a Miracle

As she began to see her situation from a new perspective, she realized that this innate feminine strength is a wonderful empowering gift to her marriage and family. What she had previously seen as "what was wrong with him," she now saw as "what was right with her." The energy between the two of them shifted as a result of this perspective change. To me, having a change of perspective is the definition of making miracles.

Susan is not alone. Over the years, men "not getting it" has been one of the most common complaints I have heard from my female clients. As women, we tend to interpret these common male tendencies as a lack of concern on their part. We very often take it personally, when in actuality, men are only lacking the ability to do what comes naturally to us as women.

We are inclined to view this masculine approach as lazy or uncaring. This is not true. Men tend to approach and process situations and feelings differently than we do. Once Susan understood this, she was able to feel a new sense of empowerment in her marriage. She began to see that when she initiated necessary discussions, she was bringing a tremendous contribution to the well-being of their relationship.

Unconsciously, Susan had needed her husband to be like her so she could feel valuable. Since, as a man, Susan's husband was unlikely and ultimately incapable of emulating her innate feminine qualities, she began to resent him and feel undervalued, unappreciated.

I believe this is one of the main reasons many women come to resent men so often. When we accept that our sense of value has to come from within ourselves, and when we recognize our distinctly feminine power as one of our greatest assets, only then will we stop searching in vain for validation from the men in our lives.

My hope is that women everywhere will identify and own their innate wisdom as an incredible gift to access, and experience authentic empowerment.

Reflections:

1. *What do you see as the uniquely feminine gifts that you bring to your relationships with others, especially men?*
2. *Do you value these gifts or take them for granted?*
3. *After reading this chapter, are you able to better understand and appreciate the differences between men and women? Do you feel resistance to this? If so, what is the resistance about and to whom is it directed?*
4. *Can you relate to Susan. What is it like to think differently about your role in your relationship? How do you imagine your relationship with your spouse/partner would be different if you did so?*

Chapter 3

If Women Were In Charge

Back in the Day...

During the late 60s, one of my mom's friends was going through a divorce. Divorce was unusual at the time, especially in our very Catholic community.

My mom and her lady friends were astonished when they heard from this friend that she wasn't able to get a credit card in her own name even though she had been the one who managed the household money, and she and her husband had excellent credit scores. She was told that because she was a woman she wasn't eligible to coattail on her ex-husband's credit. That she didn't count on her own.

My mother and her friends were shocked at the reality of what was going on in the 50s, 60s, and early 70s. These were the same women who had feared and resented the women's movement and this was a wake-up call for them. They now realized that simply because they were women, they did not have the same rights as men.

These were the same women who viewed the women's movement as an effort that would ruin families, and naively believed the world they lived in would always take care of them no matter what. They began to witness friends and family members becoming widows and divorcees.

It was then that these same women began to see things differently. They saw that female family members and friends didn't make as much money as the men they worked with, even if they did the same or sometimes more difficult work in order to feed their children. They heard stories of unfairness, sexism and sexual harassment when these women had to enter the workplace to support their families. Women were beginning to wake up and speak up. The enormity of this change was yet to be seen.

In 1974, I got a job waitressing to help pay for college. The second day on the job, the boss stuck his hand up my skirt. I found out later that this was an initiation ritual for all new waitresses. It was definitely the norm at this restaurant!

Even when I told my family, they reacted casually, suggesting I tell my boss I had six brothers who would show up if he didn't leave me alone. If these incidents happened today, I would probably own his restaurant by the time we were finished in court!

It was also common during this time for girls to be acquaintance-raped and never tell anyone because it didn't occur to them that it was rape, even when they said no and cried and resisted like hell. Letting a boy kiss you doesn't mean he can do whatever he wants, but no one told us this. Women of my generation were taught to think it was your fault if you were in that situation.

These types of assaults weren't talked about at that time; it wasn't in the realm of consciousness. I know women of my generation who didn't tell anyone about being raped or molested for over 20 years, and I'm sure there are plenty that have never told a soul.

Today, the idea that a boy or man is "entitled" to your body is absurd to most women… as it should be. This knowledge, thankfully, is part of our new, evolved, collective consciousness.

Thank God Things Have Changed

Today, as part of most college freshman orientations, there are educational awareness programs on the issue of campus sexual assault. Unfortunately, women are still being sexually assaulted, and at an appalling rate. A recent study funded by the U.S. Department of Justice found that sexual assault and stalking of college females is widespread and grossly underestimated:

- About 3% of female college students are raped during each academic year. Over the course of five calendar years, including summers and vacations, 20-25% may be raped.

– Nationally, an additional 15.5% of college females are sexually victimized (meaning sexual contact is completed with force or threat of non-physical force, threat of rape, or threat of contact).

Wow. Thank God we are now talking about this issue. Women are presently able to support each other in ways that were unavailable and unthinkable in the past. Most women who experience assault now at the very least know (whether they are able to reach out for help or not) there are resources available and they are not alone. This is a way we can have a sense of power.

This isn't only a female issue. This is really about abuse of power. When I was in high school, I heard my brothers and other boys talk about some of the priests who were at the parish and schools. They openly talked about how these guys were known to be "weirdos" or "pervs." Parents would either laugh it off or tell them not to be disrespectful. Few adults thought to ask what was going on. Now, all these years later, we know.

Being "In Charge" Doesn't Equal "Running Things"

Shortly after the U.S. war in Iraq began, I put together a workshop called "Creating A World We Would Love," and joked with friends and colleagues that the subtitle was "If Women Were In Charge." Whenever I shared the workshop title, most people would respond in an interested manner.

However, when I told them the subtitle their reactions shifted dramatically and positively. Whether I was speaking to a friend, colleague, client, there was always a "yes!" response. It was clear from their excited reactions to this subtitle that it spoke loudly to their collective appreciation of these words. Even men would have similar reactions.

During this time, I had a meeting with my marketing team. When I told them about the feedback I was getting on the workshop, they (being the marketing wizards they are) suggested I invert the title and subtitle. It came to be "If Women Were In Charge: Creating a World We Would Love."

Throughout our meeting, one of the men kept referring to the title as "If Women Were Running Things." Several times, I reminded him that it was "If women were IN CHARGE." He kept forgetting, and I began to feel more and more agitated with him each time. On my way home from the meeting, I reflected on why I was having this unusual reaction to this man's referencing the title this way. That wasn't like me. What was the big deal, I asked myself?

Then I got it! I called him and said, "I know now why it bugged me so much that you kept referring to the title as 'If Women Were Running Things.' It's because we already do!" Women are the ones who keep everything running. Homes, churches, corporations, schools, hospitals, you name it we run it.

However we are not the ones "in charge." We have had a disproportionate amount of responsibility compared to the authority we hold. And it made me wonder WHY. It is so easy to blame men, but as I acknowledged in an earlier chapter, that doesn't work. Perhaps it was appropriate during the early stages of the women's movement, but not any more.

A New Norm

No longer, as women, do we need to fight as hard to have power. We are now—and have been for some time—admitted into medical and law schools at the same rate as men. We are now able to be athletes and have the equipment and support necessary to compete at schools because of Title IX. There are now women in the military, in police headquarters, in congress, in boardrooms, science labs, pulpits and even in outer space. We have been training to be able to do jobs that were limited to men for centuries.

When I listen to younger women who take all of these rights for granted, I sometimes feel like the grandparent who says, "In our day, we walked 10 miles to school in the snow. Uphill. Both ways." I am part of that older generation who had to speak up. I was viewed as a big rebel just because I wanted to be an altar server at mass. Today, it is normal for girls to be servers at most Catholic churches (although, we still cannot be priests!), just like it's the norm for females to have the rights I've listed above.

When anyone goes through change, there is a process we undertake that leads us to a new status quo, a new norm. The new norm is here. Women and minorities are no longer left out of the boardroom. Incredibly, Barack Obama, an African American, is president. And as I write this, Hillary

Clinton is the retired Secretary of State and touted as the presumptive candidate for the next presidential campaign. Who would've ever thought!?

Evolution and Higher Consciousness

Since the 80s, we've witnessed droves of people, especially women, making a journey of spiritual, personal or physical transformation—primarily women who watched the Oprah Winfrey show. Oprah and her show represented the evolution of women and power in our society.

I believe Oprah Winfrey is a manifestation, a symbol, of a new higher level of consciousness and a new way of owning power for women and our world. *Higher Consciousness* is about being enlightened. It is about being awake and present to a deeper part of yourself, deeper than what is on the surface. Higher consciousness is about connecting to one's spirit and understanding what is really important in life. Higher consciousness is about awareness and evolution.

Because there were already many of us evolving, Oprah was able to become OPRAH! As a society, we were ready to receive this global message from someone like her. We were ready for a leader like her to emerge to lead legions of women to a new level of growth and evolution. And we were now able to see the dysfunction and abuse that kept the disenfranchised wounded, stuck and disempowered. We are now headed to an even higher level of evolution. Women are stronger, more successful and better prepared to lead the way to a healthier world.

The Angel Network

Several years ago, I watched an episode of the Oprah Winfrey Show about her Christmas visit to Africa. During this trip she saw thousands of children impacted by the AIDS epidemic. Watching this episode, I was overwhelmed with emotion, as were millions of her viewers.

Her cameras captured videos of vast numbers of children impacted by unimaginable poverty and death as a result of AIDS. We were introduced to children dying from AIDS themselves, children saying goodbye to their dying mothers, and children as young as eight and 10 years old having to raise their younger siblings in ragged, tattered tents without adults to assist them. We observed little girls and babies who had been raped because the men in this culture believe that having sex with a virgin is a way to avoid the AIDS virus.

As a result of this episode, Oprah's TV viewers were moved to help. Oprah's "Angel Network" sprang into action. They sent massive amounts of money and prayers to support her efforts in changing the lives of these afflicted children. As we know, Oprah's audience and fans have mostly consisted of women.

The following Christmas, Oprah revisited Africa. In the new footage we witnessed how the children, previously too poor to afford the school uniforms necessary to attend class, were now proudly wearing their new uniforms and attending new schools built as a result of the influx of financial support given the previous year by the Angel Network. Oprah personally funded the construction of a new all-girls school. Just one year later, these children described feeling a new sense of hope as a result of the loving care they were receiving from the Angel Network.

The follow-up segment also profiled two women ("real life angels") who were so inspired by the original segment that they had gone to Africa to nurse, teach and assist. Most audience members and viewers were hard pressed not to find themselves in tears.

These tears were twofold. Many were shed in despair over the horrifying consequences of the ongoing destitution and poverty in Africa. Others were shed as an expression of joy for the good work and generosity of so many. Countless women contributed to building a new infrastructure for the future and, in turn, created a sense of hope.

Women Will Have to Be the Ones to Change the World

Oprah ended this episode with a revered guest. He is man of extraordinary presence, a true statesman: Archbishop Desmond Tutu. As he began to speak, a most amazing thing happened. Instead of engaging in discussion with Oprah, Archbishop Tutu looked right out into the mostly female audience and, to paraphrase, said: *YOU women will have to be the ones to change the world. We men have had our chance and have made a mess.*

He went on to say that women KNOW what it is that matters, what's really important in life, and that the survival and health of our world specifically depends on women starting a revolution and making vital changes during this critical time in our history. As he spoke these words, I felt a bolt of lightning-like energy shoot down my back. Feeling deeply inspired, I knew he was right. I felt a calling deep within, and I knew I had to take action. I was sitting on my couch in my pajamas, watching TV before going to bed. That was the moment of conception for this book.

I knew that Archbishop Tutu was absolutely right. I began to think about how often I had read a story in the paper or saw something on the news and I'd think, "If women were in charge, this would be different." I especially think this whenever I see the realities of war, or when a convicted wife beater, pedophile, rapist or murderer gets sentenced to short terms in prison only to brutalize, rape, or kill again; when a homicidal drunk driver walks away with community service, while some kid caught with pot in his car gets thrown in prison for years.

How Things Could be Different if Women Were in Charge

I think about how it might be if women were in charge of the criminal justice system. I fantasize about how things would be different. I imagine that, if women were in charge, our legal system would be totally revamped; it would actually be fair and just. I think about the possibilities for our political system as well. If women were in charge, I envision governing and policy-making that really is "by the people and for the people."

Continuing my fantasy, I imagine a world without war. Regardless of your politics, it's hard to believe we'd have so many wars if women were in charge. Killing, especially killing children, is innately foreign to a woman's sensibility. As women, we know that even the toughest career soldier is someone's child.

In fact, when we hear about female suicide bombers, it horrifies us even more than when it's a man committing this egregious act. We know that something is incredibly and inherently broken when a woman creates such violence. It scares us to our deepest core when something so unnatural happens in our world.

Envision a World Where Women Were in Charge

What if women were in charge of healthcare? How would things be different? Would women be forced to leave the hospital the day after they gave birth? Would babies in need of neonatal care be discharged in five to six days when experienced, smart, wise nurses like my sister-in-law Tara know they should be there four to five weeks?

What if women were in charge of the business world, the quality of daycare, education, the environment and religion? These are issues we all must address because they impact the whole of our society in the short and long term.

I believe that our systems, societies and world would work in a much more peaceful and effective way because it would stem from the inherent spirit inside most women, which is that of collaboration and cooperation. Confronted by life's challenges and global situations, we often feel frustrated, concerned, and helpless, wondering what difference we could possibly make.

Lately, every time I read a magazine or a newspaper or turn on the news, I see and hear more and more examples that continue to affirm the importance of my question: "How would this be handled if women were in charge and able to find more heart-centered solutions?"

It's Beginning to Happen

Marianne Williamson, a Unity Church minister, renowned speaker and author of many books, recently ran for congress in California. She had to confront the status quo of both of the major political parties in our country. Here is a blurb from her website about why she ran for office (how's this for Feminine Heart Energy?):

> "If elected to Congress, I will take a stand for human values, not
> economic ones, as the ordering principle of our society. I will
> promote a politics of conscience and a new bottom line. I will put
> the health and wellbeing of our children above the health and
> wellbeing of Wall Street. I will add my voice to the movement
> supporting a Constitutional Amendment outlawing the undue

influence of money on our politics, and foster a more enlightened perspective about America and our role in the world today."

If you are not already familiar with the name Malala Yousafzai, you will most likely be hearing it as time goes on. Diane Sawyer did a fascinating interview with this amazing teenager in the fall of 2013. Malala is a 17-year-old girl from Pakistan. She has written a book about her journey called *I am Malala*.

In October 2012, there was an assassination attempt on her. She was shot in the head by the Taliban because she had been advocating education for girls. (The Taliban bans girls from attending schools.)

Incredibly, she survived and has become an activist for the right of all children to receive an education. Her philosophy is that education is the pathway to peace. Not only was she named one of *Time* magazine's 100 most influential people in the world, she also spoke to the UN and called for worldwide access to education. In 2014 Malala Yousafzai won the Nobel Peace Prize. She is the youngest person to win it. All this from a 17-year-old who has felt called to make a difference and owned her power with her courage and her words.

Reflections:

1. *If you ruled the world and could change one thing, what would that be?*
2. *Where do you most want to make a difference?*
3. *Are there areas in your life where you have the responsibility but not the authority? What would need to happen for you to have the authority, and would you be comfortable with it?*

Chapter 4

The Prize in the Cracker Jack Box, or Authentic vs. Illusionary Power

You don't have to have seen an episode of the Oprah Winfrey show, or read a self-help book, or been in therapy or participated in a 12 step program reading to relate to this book. It is relevant to you because you are here, now, on this planet. You are part of families, businesses, religious communities, neighborhoods, towns and countries that need women who "get it." We are women of wisdom, and it's time for us to recognize that authentic empowerment is neither acting like men nor "acting" to manipulate men. That is an old pre-feminist model, which is based on women being passive, submissive and unquestioning.

Power for women of this patriarchal era meant being manipulative. Mothers actually taught their daughters to always let men win even if they were capable of beating them; dumb down, don't show how smart you are, especially if you are smarter than them; act helpless so men can feel competent and manly; put up with bad behavior as a way to keep a man.

Having power meant "catching" a man who had power and means. (The movie *Titanic* portrayed this antiquated mindset perfectly.) We then evolved from this mindset to finding our way into a man's world by imitating male empowerment. It was a necessary part of the process of getting to where we are presently.

21

Now imagine the next stage in our development and how powerful we will be when we quit emulating and start leading, integrating our wisdom with the knowledge we've learned by being in the world and now knowing and understanding its infrastructure!

As women, we tend to lead from our hearts. But how often do we identify this as a real, valid and critical resource to help heal the world? How often do we instead discount this gift we possess? It's critical to intentionally and purposefully contribute your Feminine Heart Energy to a world that desperately needs healing, and that desperately needs leaders acting from a place of higher consciousness. You will also learn how to thrive as a heart-centered woman who understands the calling for the revolution Archbishop Tutu asked us to undertake.

I invite, encourage and challenge you, women of all ages and nationalities, to realize your personal potential and to use your unique wisdom as THE power to transform the world.

While we no longer have the Oprah Winfrey show to enlighten and inspire us, I believe that we no longer need the Oprah Winfrey show. Twenty-five years of her leadership has helped women and men throughout the world acquire and download the software required for the next generation of change. Oprah's show existed because we women were ready for a new awakening. She was a manifestation of our readiness as women, and as a culture, for truth and a healthier sense of power.

Oprah created a venue to assist us in becoming our best selves. She was clear that this was her role and purpose in her life. Her gift was to motivate, teach and encourage her audience. She was intentional in making choices that enabled her to facilitate her purpose. Oprah is known to be a strong and successful businesswoman. I once heard her tell an interviewer that she never made career decisions based on money, only based on what felt like the right thing to do. In other words, she listened to her heart. What an evolved mindset for success! And what success she has attained. Perhaps she's on to something!

As you can see, when Oprah was called to the place God wanted, her deep gladness met the deep needs of the world. A big thanks to Oprah for putting her Feminine Heart Energy out into the world and leading the revolution of our evolution. Now it's time to upgrade to the next generation, which we can't do if we don't have "authentic" power.

What is Illusionary Power?

Let's talk about authentic power and what it is and is not. We know that it's NOT behaving like men. This is the part of the book that men in particular are really going to like. Ladies, I am inviting you to re-evaluate the behaviors and attitudes that tend to keep us stuck as women in our quest for power.

Here's a list of identifying behaviors and characteristics that occur when we experience illusionary power:

1. Your main way of communicating your needs (especially with a spouse) is cajoling, bitching, nagging or manipulating. This means spending an enormous amount of time and energy attempting to get them to "get it" in order to feel validated. You have a difficult time accepting others and situations for what they are, instead of what you want them to be. You aren't interested in understanding where others are coming from, and only want them to be on the same page as you. You don't "get it" when others "don't get it."

2. You have difficulty being honest with yourself and others. As a result, you tend to act out of fear and desperation. Gossiping, backstabbing, competitiveness, drama and conflict tend to drive your relationships.

3. You do not have healthy boundaries. Your boundaries tend to be too rigid, too loose or nonexistent. You're inclined to expect others to read your mind, feeling resentment when others don't magically know or meet your needs. You equate love with holding someone emotionally hostage ("If you loved me...).''

4. You rationalize, deny and minimize dysfunctional situations. You make excuses for your unhealthy behavior as well as that of others. Because you have difficulty being honest, and taking responsibility for yourself, you frequently project uncomfortable feelings about the self on to others.

You also have problems accepting unwanted consequences. Self-delusion, fantasy and regressive thinking are not uncommon.

5. Very often, you feel helpless, afraid, overwhelmed, depressed, hopeless and angry. You may tend to express feelings in inappropriate and controlling ways, blaming others, denying feelings, acting out or somatizing.

6. You fear change, and see it as a threat rather than a natural part of life. As a result, you develop a controlling personality and an inability to feel peaceful on a regular basis.

7. You can't trust yourself. You don't have the skills and emotional infrastructure to handle life as a mature adult. Unable to differentiate intuition from impulsiveness and magical thinking, you feel and behave in obsessive/compulsive ways on a regular basis. You adopt an "all or nothing" approach to life, tending to be either very indulgent or depriving with yourself and others.

8. Your thinking is, more often than not, negative. You are quick to criticize and judge. You tend to be unable to see options.

9. You experience life's challenges as problems that are unsolvable. You tend to stay stuck and unable to see any options for change and growth. You cannot think outside the box and have a tendency to see the glass as half empty. It is a challenge for you to experience gratitude; therefore you rarely express it.

10. You lack a real sense of purpose in life. You have an immature perception of God, and low consciousness. You tend to be spiritually disinterested, disconnected or rigidly fundamental. You look outside yourself for a sense of purpose and identity, giving away your power to external factors. You see "signs" as being only coincidences, and are unable to look beyond the material world.

11. You are unable (or afraid) to own and appreciate your sense of self and purpose in healthy, appropriate ways. You're consistently self-deprecating, tending to be obsessive and critical of your body. You minimize or over-idealize your roles, relationships with self and others, gifts and talents. You aren't able to view yourself as an expression of Divine light and love.

12. Your energy is ungrounded, chaotic, draining, frantic or shut-down. You suck energy from others or allow others to suck it from you. You're unable to experience a sense of cooperation within self and with others. You are in competition with others from sense of insecurity, lack or scarcity.

Now that we've identified the "old" dysfunctional ways we've tended to have power, let's look at a list of characteristics and behaviors we experience when we have authentic power. If this book were a Cracker Jack box this would be the prize! It's the "how to" part where you can actually gauge the authenticity of your power through your relationships with self and others.

I encourage you to copy this list, keep it in your day planner, and refer to it often to assist you in making changes to strengthen your sense of true power. When you live this way on a consistent basis you will begin to experience peace, harmony and love in a way that words don't even begin to express. You will understand the power of your own spirit.

Identifying Behaviors and Characteristics that Occur When We Experience Authentic Power:

1. Your main way of communicating is to be direct and honest, without judgment. You have the ability to speak your truth, the self discipline and inner wisdom to wait until it is the right time and circumstance to do so, and are able to so without an emotional attachment to outcome and judgment.

2. You accept people and situations for who/what they are. You recognize and honor limitations of self and others. You "get it" when others "don't get it." You accept people for who they are instead of who you want them to be.

3. You have healthy boundaries. You have a clear sense of being separate, and yet connected. You are able to request what you need, and accept and respect when someone else cannot meet your needs.

4. You are able to take responsibility for yourself. You can be honest when you screw up, and are also able to hold others accountable when they screw up. When others hurt you, you look at your own part in whatever circumstances took place, and are able to accept the consequences that occur as a result of your behavior.

5. You experience your own feelings and those of others without judgment. In spite of ups and downs, you are consistently able to feel an underlying sense of peacefulness, and an overall sense of well-being, happiness and contentment.

6. You welcome change as an opportunity for growth. You appreciate and celebrate differences. You're open and willing to let go of old ways and traditions that no longer work, even when it's scary. You're able to see change as natural part of life.

7. You are consistently in tune with your intuition. You allow it to be a major guide in life and making informed decisions, along with the feedback of others.

8. You have the ability to forgive yourself and others. You do the work needed to come to a place of forgiveness, not just give lip service. You give others the benefit of the doubt.

9. You utilize challenges in life as a way to connect to spiritual growth and purpose. You are able to turn pain into gain. Experiencing and expressing gratitude, love and appreciation are a normal part of life. You tend to focus on the positive—seeing the glass as half full. You're able to be creative in problem solving.

10. You experience life from a place of cooperation rather than competition. You're conscious about universal cooperation and look to external events to support your decision-making. You are able to know there are always options even when they aren't obvious at the time, and you ask for help when needed.

11. You recognize, and are ready and willing, to own a sense of self and purpose. You're consistently able to validate, appreciate, respect and celebrate your own gifts, talents and body. You have the ability to communicate this self-knowledge as part of your being an expression of Divine light and love on this earth, and are willing to be an inspiration to others.

12. Your energy and life force is grounded, loving, attractive and enriching to be around. Others are attracted to being around you. You consistently experience a sense of security from within. You feel a spirit of cooperation within yourself and behave accordingly with others. You know how to direct, transform and use energy, and, to recognize this as a way of having Higher Consciousness.

The next section shows the characteristics and qualities of both Illusionary Power and Authentic Power in a table format, side by side, so you may easily compare and contrast them for yourself. This tool provides a compass for assessing your own behavior so you can get a sense, at any given time, of whether you are operating from a place of authentic power or not. It provides a context for checking in with yourself. Reflections at the end of this chapter will help you look inward and attain a more clear understanding of yourself and how you own your power.

Illusionary Power	Authentic Power
1. Your main way of communicating your needs (especially with a spouse) is cajoling, bitching, nagging or manipulating. This means spending an enormous amount of time and energy attempting to get them to "get it" in order to feel validated. You have a difficult time accepting others and situations for what they are, instead of what you want them to be. You aren't interested in understanding where others are coming from, and only want them to be on the same page as you. You don't "get it" when others "don't get it."	**1. Your main way of communicating is to be direct and honest, without judgment.** You have the ability to speak your truth, the self discipline and inner wisdom to wait until it is the right time and circumstance to do so, and are able to so without an emotional attachment to outcome and judgment.
2. You have difficulty being honest with yourself and others. As a result, you tend to act out of fear and desperation. Gossiping, backstabbing, competitiveness, drama and conflict tend to drive your relationships.	**2. You accept people and situations for who/what they are.** You recognize and honor limitations of self and others. You "get it" when others "don't get it." You accept people for who they are instead of who you want them to be.
3. You do not have healthy boundaries. Your boundaries tend to be too rigid, too loose or nonexistent. You're inclined to expect others to read your mind, feeling resentment when others don't magically know or meet your needs. You equate love with holding someone emotionally hostage ("If you loved me...").	**3. You have healthy boundaries.** You have a clear sense of being separate, and yet connected. You are able to request what you need, and accept and respect when someone else cannot meet your needs.

Illusionary Power	Authentic Power
4. **You rationalize, deny and minimize dysfunctional situations.** You make excuses for your unhealthy behavior as well as that of others. Because you have difficulty being honest, and taking responsibility for yourself, you frequently project uncomfortable feelings about the self on to others. You also have problems accepting unwanted consequences. Self-delusion, fantasy and regressive thinking are not uncommon.	4. **You are able to take responsibility for yourself.** You can be honest when you screw up, and are also able to hold others accountable when they screw up. When others hurt you, you look at your own part in whatever circumstances took place, and are able to accept the consequences that occur as a result of your behavior.
5. **Very often, you feel helpless, afraid, overwhelmed, depressed, hopeless and angry.** You may tend to express feelings in inappropriate and controlling ways, blaming others, denying feelings, acting out or somatizing.	5. **You experience your own feelings and those of others without judgment.** In spite of ups and downs, you are consistently able to feel an underlying sense of peacefulness, and an overall sense of well-being, happiness and contentment.
6. **You fear change, and see it as a threat rather than a natural part of life.** As a result, you develop a controlling personality and an inability to feel peaceful on a regular basis.	6. **You welcome change as an opportunity for growth.** You appreciate and celebrate differences. You're open and willing to let go of old ways and traditions that no longer work, even when it's scary. You're able to see change as a natural part of life.

Illusionary Power	Authentic Power
7. You can't trust yourself. You don't have the skills and emotional infrastructure to handle life as a mature adult. Unable to differentiate intuition from impulsiveness and magical thinking, you feel and behave in obsessive/compulsive ways on a regular basis. You adopt an "all or nothing" approach to life, tending to be either very indulgent or depriving, with yourself and others.	**7. You are consistently in tune with your intuition.** You allow it to be a major guide in life and making informed decisions, along with the feedback of others.
8. Your thinking is, more often than not, negative. You are quick to criticize and judge. You tend to be unable to see options.	**8. You have the ability to forgive yourself and others.** You do the work needed to come to a place of forgiveness, not just give lip service. You give others the benefit of the doubt.
9. You experience life's challenges as problems that are unsolvable. You tend to stay stuck and unable to see any options for change and growth. You cannot think outside the box and have a tendency to see the glass as half empty. It is a challenge for you to experience gratitude; therefore you rarely express it.	**9. You utilize challenges in life as a way to connect to spiritual growth and purpose.** You are able to turn pain into gain. Experiencing and expressing gratitude, love and appreciation are a normal part of life. You tend to focus on the positive— seeing the glass as half full. You're able to be creative in problem solving.

Illusionary Power	Authentic Power
10. You lack a real sense of purpose in life. You have an immature perception of God, and low consciousness. You tend to be spiritually disinterested, disconnected or rigidly fundamental. You look outside yourself for a sense of purpose and identity, giving away your power to external factors. You see "signs" as being only coincidences, and are unable to look beyond the material world.	**10. You experience life from a place of cooperation rather than competition.** You're conscious about universal cooperation and look to external events to support your decision-making. You are able to know there are always options even when they aren't obvious at the time, and you ask for help when needed.
11. You are unable (or afraid) to own and appreciate your sense of self and purpose in healthy, appropriate ways. You're consistently self-deprecating, tending to be obsessive and critical of your body. You minimize or over-idealize your roles, relationships with self and others, gifts and talents. You see expressing yourself as expressions of God's light and love as being prideful.	**11. You recognize, and are ready and willing, to own a sense of self and purpose.** You're consistently able to validate, appreciate, respect and celebrate your own gifts, talents and body. You have the ability to communicate this self-knowledge as part of your being an expression of Divine light and love on this earth, and are willing to be an inspiration to others.

Illusionary Power	Authentic Power
12. **Your energy is ungrounded, chaotic, draining, frantic or shut-down.** You suck energy from others or allow others to suck it from you. You're unable to experience a sense of cooperation within self and with others. You are in competition with others from sense of insecurity, lack or scarcity.	12. **Your energy and life force is grounded, loving, attractive and enriching to be around.** Others are attracted to being around you. You consistently experience a sense of security from within. You feel a spirit of cooperation within yourself and behave accordingly with others. You know how to direct, transform and use energy, and, to recognize this as a way of having Higher Consciousness.

Reflections:

1. *In what areas of your life do you feel stuck or experience problems? Using your journal and the illusionary vs. authentic power table provided above, ask yourself: How do I tend to communicate and handle challenges and problems in my life? Do I typically utilize authentic or illusionary ways of dealing with these situations?*

2. *What areas of my life work well? Using the illusionary vs. authentic power table again, ask yourself: "How do I typically communicate and handle the areas of my life that work well? Do I use authentic or illusionary means of dealing with situations I am comfortable and happy with, like my job, spouse, kids or friends?*

3. *What are the differences between the answers to questions 2 and 3? What authentic power behavior could you use as a means to change how you relate to the challenging situations and people in your life? Which ones would you use, and in what specific situations?*

4. *Do your behaviors and attitudes toward yourself and others reflect these values? How so, or how not?*

Chapter 5

The Heart of The Matter: Feminine Heart Energy

My client Christina is a boldly competent woman. Some might refer to her as a force with which to be reckoned. She is a great example of someone who transitioned from a sense of illusionary power into authentic heart-centered power. Christina's story demonstrates how this impacted her relationship not only with herself, but also with her family. Christina has four children, three of whom are grown in their 20's, and she has been married for over 30 years to a man who most people would agree is a pretty great guy. For most of their marriage, though, he drove her nuts because he didn't do things the way she thought they should be done.

When I first met Christina she told me she was, in her own words, a great example of someone who was "tough." She reported rarely showing her feelings unless it was anger or frustration. Christina's idea of having power was to nag, complain and push. She spent years attempting to control her family at most turns. Her solutions, when they worked, were temporary at best and rarely satisfying for her or her family. But still she kept trying. She was chronically in power struggles with her husband or children, and often felt angry, resentful and alone. Christina's husband and kids tended to be very passive-aggressive or overly emotional in their power struggle with her.

In spite of her best efforts and concern for the well-being of her family, her forceful style created the opposite effect of what she'd intended.

In Christina's attempts to get her family to listen to her advice and help them succeed in life, her family shut her out. They rarely listened to her, saw her as a "bitch," and treated her with little respect or concern. This, of course, infuriated her more.

Then Christina was diagnosed with heart disease. This was the impetus for her to start therapy and, as a result, began to heal the part of herself that led her to be such a controlling person in the first place. Recently, she was facing yet another surgery. She'd just had surgery a few months previously, and her post-op recovery had been a disaster. Christina was seeing a spiritual director, who spoke to her about her past surgery experience. The spiritual director suggested they pray together and set the intention that the nurses, doctors and aids for the upcoming surgery would be very caring and competent. Christina kept holding on to this image in meditations prior to this surgery.

Opening Your Heart is a Powerful Act of Courage

Thankfully, Christina reported that her experience this time was wonderful. In fact, she told me how excited she was to see that all this theory she'd been reading about how to own power from a place of faith rather than force (a product of fear) really worked. She began to understand how to have a more authentic sense of power in how she approached things, whether it be surgery or her family. She was able to be soft and openhearted with her son, inviting him to go to therapy together to try to work out conflict they'd had with each other from a recently disastrous family party.

Christina allowed herself to be vulnerable with her son and showed her pain about their distant relationship and her fears about her illness. As a result, she created an opportunity for them to bond in a way both had feared impossible. When Christina learned to move TOWARD something positive (faith) instead of AWAY from something negative (fear), she was able to own her Feminine Heart Energy and find the joy and strength that occurs as a result.

For Christina, opening her heart was a powerful act of courage. Owning and sharing her Feminine Heart Energy enabled her to experience much more effective and rewarding ways of having power and love.

In spite of her "tough" demeanor, Christina had been feeling helpless because she couldn't control her family. Her transformation took place after she became ill and couldn't "control" things any more. Ironically, her heart disease provided the opportunity for her to learn how to tap into her Feminine Heart Energy.

The Importance of Balance

Although the focus of this book is Feminine Heart Energy, that doesn't mean our *thinking* ability is unimportant. Our ability to have mental clarity is incredibly important. Achieving a heart energy-focused life is about balance. I see our heart as the hinge connecting our heads (thoughts) and our bodies (feelings).

When we are born, we have no thinking ability. This is something that occurs over time as our brains develop. But all babies are born with feelings. In fact, learning how to manage feelings is a critical part of a child's developmental process.

Adults, on the other hand, tend to stay in their heads, utilizing their cognitive abilities to reason. My belief is that in order to be human beings of authentic power and of Higher Consciousness, we need to have a balance between our thoughts, our feelings and our spirit. Feminine Heart Energy is at the center of our being where the mind and body come together in "holy communion." It is the place where we are able to "see rightly." Whenever we come from our heart we come from our Highest Self, or some people call it our soul—our God voice within—our intuition. I call it Feminine Heart Energy. It is WISDOM.

A Catholic Rectory: The Perfect Training Ground for Becoming a Feminist

When I think about a woman who truly models being in Holy Communion with the human and the divine, Mary the Blessed Mother comes to mind. As far as I'm concerned, Mary wins the Feminine Heart Energy award hands down!

However, I didn't always view Mary in the kindest light. For a long time, I didn't want to be anything like her. Perhaps this has to do with reconciling my ongoing journey as a woman with my Catholic upbringing. In reflecting on my past, I can tell you that working as a young woman in the rectory (the building where Catholic priests live) at my local parish, I didn't always hold Mary in the highest regard.

I grew up in a blue-collar neighborhood. When I was in 7th grade, I got my first job. My family lived down the block from our church, and we were all very involved parishioners. My brothers were altar boys and athletes, so naturally, as a girl, I got to work at the rectory answering phones and serving dinner to priests.

But this was 1967. Things were changing dramatically in both the world and the Church. I was learning I could only do the job I had *because I wasn't a boy*. I was entering puberty and it was becoming very clear that having a penis was quite an advantage in our world.

The girls were only allowed to use the school gym if and when the boys didn't want to use it. Priests were kings of the castle, and nuns were the ladies in waiting. Yes, it was crystal clear who had the power.

One day, while entering the rectory to pick up my paycheck, a group of boys my age, all of them in sweaty basketball uniforms following their game, were hanging out with one of the priests in the office.

When he saw me walking into the rectory, he bellowed out that I needed to leave immediately. I told him I was only there to get my pay. He told me that it didn't matter—that I was not allowed in the rectory at any time in shorts. I was actually in a very cute coordinated shirt and shorts outfit, thank you very much! It was extremely hot outside, and I was just passing by to pick up my check, not to work or hang out.

But: I was a girl. When I very respectfully challenged him about the fact that these sweaty, sloppy boys in shorts were there just hanging out, I was further admonished for speaking up to a priest. I was not behaving like a "good Catholic girl." In other words, I was not behaving like Mary the Blessed Mother, who to people of the Catholic faith is regarded the ultimate role model for women. Or at least, not the way I had been taught the Blessed Mother would have behaved.

Misogynistic incidents like this one were commonplace and reinforced my aversion to Mary as the iconic figurehead of femininity for Catholics. She was supposed to be an example to young girls like me, but quite frankly, I didn't want to be anything like her.

An Angel with a Box of Books

The New Testament tells us that Mary the Blessed Mother was visited by an angel, but I was visited by a human with a box of books.

Anna Mae was a very nice woman who lived with her elderly parents. She knew I loved to read and from time to time would drop off a box of her recently read novels. For me it was like having a treasure chest show up at the door.

This was during a stage of my life when I felt very alone and confused. As a girl coming of age during the 60s, I felt disempowered and not terribly optimistic about having a fulfilling life. I wanted to know why things were they way they were. I wanted to know why boys at that time just by virtue of gender had more choices and power than girls. My mom would tell me I'd been asking questions from the time I could talk; this was not meant as a compliment.

Because I was in an environment where people were taught not to question, I suspected that perhaps something was wrong with me. My inquisitive nature and my hope for more options in life made me feel crazy and, even more so, alone. Miraculously, I was provided with the help and support I needed: that awesome box of books from Anna Mae.

To this day, I'm not sure if she has any idea what she did for me, but in one particular box were two unlikely nonfiction books now considered classics in feminist literature: *The Second Sex* by Simone de Beauvoir and *The Feminine Mystique* by Betty Friedan. I devoured them both like they were novels. These books assured me that I was not crazy and certainly not alone! I had support come to me when I needed it, from a most unexpected source, in a most unexpected way. Those books changed the direction of my life's course.

A Gift of Grace and Faith

Fast-forward 15 years: I was in Israel with a group of nuns and priests, and I was offered the opportunity to give the homily during one of the services. Honored, I accepted.

Then I found out that the scripture was the Annunciation, where an angel tells Mary, a virgin, that she is pregnant and that God is the father of this baby.

I'll be honest: When I found out that this was the piece of scripture I needed to reflect on, I was thrown for a loop. The thought of sharing my views on the Mother of Christianity in front of 42 nuns and priests rattled me. I was incredibly uncomfortable at the thought of sharing my negative impression of the ultimate woman (in the eyes of the Church) with people who had taken vows to uphold and honor her.

It was a sticky situation; I didn't want to lie, but I didn't want to be offensive, either. I knew that as someone raised Catholic, it was practically heresy to admit that I was none too enamored with Mary. However, I was not thrilled that the main role model available to me as a Catholic woman was someone who seemed, in my opinion, passive, submissive, notoriously asexual, and with no choice over her life's path.

Having grown and matured in my own spiritual development throughout my late 20's, I believed that everything happens for a reason. Trusting that there was a reason I'd been given this piece of Scripture, I meditated and asked God for help in this matter. I spent an afternoon praying to be able to see Mary with some new understanding and wisdom.

I carefully and deliberately read and reread the assigned passage. As I did, something shifted inside of me and I was able to see Mary with new eyes. I began to picture this young woman (basically still a girl) alone, pregnant, and—I imagine—very frightened. If I were her, I most likely would have thought I was certifiably insane.

That day, I began to see that Mary had the incredible ability to trust her heart to "know" that she was listening to her God-voice within. I saw her strength, love and willingness for what it was: a gift of grace and faith. This changed how I perceived Mary. I now saw her as a powerful model of Feminine Heart Energy.

That day, during my homily, I was able to share how Mary became for me the personification of a woman's ability to trust herself and her God-voice within. Mary owned her strength, which obviously has had some great staying power, and that day I gained some wisdom.

The Love Child Of Our Heart and Soul

Wisdom is defined as insight, a deep, thorough or mature understanding. It is what I would also call Higher Consciousness, but it goes by many names. It can also be called insight, knowing or intuition. I think wisdom is the love child of our heart and soul. It is an invisible force like love and, like our soul, it exists within our deepest selves. Perhaps another way to describe it is as *our essence.*

As part of our language, we use heart terminology to describe someone's deepest core. We use phrases like "at the heart of the matter" to identify the most central part of an issue. We talk about people we know as "good-hearted" or "having a great heart" to identify someone who is kind, caring and generous.

We also speak of "having the heart to do something" which means having courage, spirit, or resolution. My nephew Brian's basketball coach told his parents that he wished other kids on his team played with "as much heart" as he does because the team would be a great deal better. The heart is the nucleus of our being. Much the way the biological heart is the center of our bodies, the feminine heart is the center of our spiritual selves, and its energy is what keeps our spirit alive.

Wisdom in Action is Power

Power is the ability to take action, lead and influence. Knowing what is really important in life is what gives us wisdom. Women tend to have an innate urge to reach out to others in need no matter what the "rules" say or whose side someone is on. However, it's not enough to have this innate urge. *When we combine our innate wisdom with taking action we achieve power. It's THE power that we often don't perceive as power.*

For example: It's the soft, sensitive and compassionate strength that empowers one, even in the midst of sheer exhaustion, to be able to stay up all hours of the night with babies, to make meals or to clean the homes of sick family members and friends.

Women's innate wisdom fuels the actions behind an organization like MADD (Mothers Against Drunk Drivers), which finally got our country to take drunk driving seriously. It's someone like Cindy Sheehan, who, in her quiet determination, had the forcefulness and courage during the Iraq war to garner national attention about the loss of her child and other's children in a war she believed was unjust.

As Desmond Tutu suggested, women "get it." We understand what is really important. *Feminine Heart Energy is that which we know in our hearts to be true. Peace and love.* It's something inside of all of us, and it's in you whether you are a man or a woman.

Security Comes From Having Internal Resources.

About 15 years ago, I went on a yoga retreat. At the end of one of the classes, the students were hanging around chatting with the teacher. The words she spoke that day continue to be insightful and helpful to me.

She said she used to think her power and security came from her family, where she lived, her job, how much money she had saved and other physical things. What she came to realize was that her security did not come from those external things, but that her real power came from knowing she had the internal resources to handle whatever came along in life.

In particular, she identified her relationship with her "God within" as being her primary resource for security and power. I sensed that she had been through some rough times in her life and that she had used these experiences to develop these inner resources. She was NOT saying, nor am I, that financial, job and family security aren't important, but as the old saying goes, "money can't buy happiness." All you need to do is look at the tabloids to realize money, status and success aren't enough when something bigger than those things is missing inside.

It's Not What Happens, but How We Handle What Happens

Identifying the inner resources to guide us to deal with life's challenges is the first step for individuals wishing to achieve a healthy sense of power.

This is, in fact, what people do every day in my office. They develop and strengthen their inner resources in order to be able to handle life's challenges and manifest whatever external resources they need. Having these inner resources—the skills and tools to deal with life—is crucial for our well-being.

As the yoga teacher reminded us, external resources can be here today and gone tomorrow. All the money and success in the world cannot provide a true sense of power. The difference between having an authentic or false sense of power is not about what happens to you, but how you handle what happens. Authentic power comes from having the inner resources necessary to meet life's challenges. Our inner resources are the ultimate money in the bank and money in the bank is a way to have power.

Owning Our Power

I believe women in particular have amazing wisdom and inner resources. We have big bank accounts.

Unfortunately, in spite of having a big "bank account" we often act like the old lady who dies living in poverty but who has hundreds of thousands of dollars hidden in her mattress. We can't afford to be that lady. It is important that we recognize that it is WE who have the tools and skills necessary to address the serious challenges that presently face our world.

In order to transform the world into a place we would love, we have to first see ourselves as the ones who hold the power and means to create these needed changes. This means loving ourselves and valuing our natural gifts.

When we embrace our inner resources, and trust our natural ways of knowing, then, we can put what we know to use. *This* is owning our power. We can show the world how to create miracles by sharing our wisdom, our "know-how."

A newly evolved generation of power comes from truly valuing our innate wisdom and the inherent differences we bring to the table as women—*not* from thinking and behaving like men. It is time to stop equating power with traditional masculine thought and behavior. Those days need to be over if we are ever going to create a world we would love.

Man-Kind

Things are changing. More men are involved in parenting than ever before. More "successful" men are quitting stressful jobs to spend more time with their families. More men, once they've raised their families, are leaving highly paid jobs they don't like to become teachers and volunteers, and to take other low-paying but rewarding jobs. Thankfully more men are embracing roles that have traditionally belonged to women.

In general, men—especially the younger generations—seem to be less sexist (not counting some musicians), more accepting of women bosses in the workplace, and more accepting of women having power. Thankfully more men are better at expressing their feelings and showing physical affection than any previous generation.

Two examples of prominent men who appear to be integrating their Feminine Heart Energy with their resources, experience and knowledge are President Bill Clinton and philanthropist billionaire Bill Gates. They have used their high profiles as well as their hearts, financial power and connections to become ambassadors for change on a global scale.

The work of the Clinton Family Foundation includes providing resources to assist with the issue areas of climate control, economic development, global health, health and wellness, and women and girls.

Like Clinton, Bill Gates along with his wife Melina have also created a foundation that focuses on education, healthcare and women. They are doing things that are feminine in nature—reaching out to others in need and strongly recognizing the need for women to become more empowered.

Obviously, these men are in a different league than most people in our society. But many less-powerful men are reaching out as well. The guys who coach their kids, do volunteer work in their community and show up for their families every day are expressing their Feminine Heart Energy.

There are many wonderful men connecting to their feminine side, providing service and kindness every day. I should know—I see them regularly in my office, and am honored to have male family members and friends who demonstrate loving-kindness on a regular basis.

The Tuna Casserole Brigade

When the horrific events of 9/11 happened, we had a chance to look deep into ourselves as Americans and examine our role in the world. It was an opportunity for a wake-up call, a time to recognize what is really important in life. There was a softening of hearts throughout our country. It was an incredibly sad, poignant, yet in some ways beautiful time, as Americans from all over the country reached out to the three sites that were violently attacked, with tremendous assistance, support and openheartedness. People from all over the world also reached out to our country with care and generosity. New York City in particular was showered with loving-kindness.

Throughout this time there was a level of higher consciousness in our awareness and appreciation for one another, for the fire, police, medical personnel and for our government officials. As a nation we became what I like to call the "Tuna Casserole Brigade." It was a time when people opened their hearts and connected with the energy that enabled them to do what women do naturally day in and day out in much smaller, yet incredibly meaningful ways.

How many of you know someone who has been sick with cancer, brought home a newborn, experienced a death in the family or found themselves caring for an elderly parent, and discovered dinner ready and waiting from friends, neighbors, church groups, moms from your kids' school, or women from your book club? Who is it that takes turns babysitting, or making sure the house is clean when you come home from the hospital?

Women. These acts of kindness and nurturing come naturally from women. There doesn't have to be a worldwide disaster involving hundreds or thousands of people for us to know how to be a good friend and neighbor.

As women, we innately tune into the world around us. We take the gift of relationship seriously, make connections to everyone around us more meaningful, and for the most part, do it without even thinking. This is not to say men aren't kind, thoughtful and generous… just that it's not the same. You aren't going to find many men bringing brownies or cake to the office because they know it's someone's birthday!

What happens when we take seriously the value of this innate gift of heart energy? That our "knowing" is so automatic almost fools us into not recognizing the authentic power it has. Imagine what will happen when we do!

Reflections:

1. Have you ever had a "Mary" experience, when you were able to see the same situation from a new perspective?
2. Can you identify what your inner resources are? How do you apply them in your life? What are the external resources that are available? Do you use them in ways that are in alignment with your values?
3. Do you see yourself as someone who has integrated both external (education, experience, time, money) and internal (sense of self, confidence, spiritual foundation, emotionally stable) resources? If not, what part(s) require work and what can you do to create what you need?
4. In what ways do you take yourself for granted?

Chapter 6

What's Energy Got To Do With It?

In the previous chapter, Christina's story exemplified this quote: "A miracle is being able to see the same thing from a new perspective." These words of wisdom were spoken by Fr. Don Senior, a renown scripture scholar and one of the finest teachers I've ever had.

More than 30 years later, these powerful words still resonate with me and serve as the basis for both this book and the work I do as a psychotherapist. Ultimately, this book is about redefining power. In other words: being able to see power from a new perspective. As we discussed previously, Archbishop Tutu challenged us women to tap into our innate wisdom and utilize it as a powerful means to transform our world. I believe that in order to do so, it is imperative we look at what power means from a fresh viewpoint. This involves learning how to own, identify and access our energy and power in more evolved and abundant ways than ever before.

As I began writing this book, I realized I could not talk about power without first talking about energy. Without energy there is no power.

Because so often energy is an unseen force, it is challenging to describe what I mean when I use the terms "power" and "energy," and to be able to identify the distinction between the two.

Here's a start: Energy is what fuels power. The only way to have power is to have energy. Consciously identifying, owning and utilizing one's energy is crucial to creating authentic power.

Energy is a term used to describe many things; in some ways it is similar to the word love. We understand both love and energy as part of our collective human experience. There are various physical expressions of each, but their definitions are diverse and often elusive. I frequently find it difficult to discuss energy in a concrete manner that makes clear sense and doesn't sound too *flaky*. Comprehending what energy is, how it works, how it is related to having power and how to utilize it is the cornerstone of this book.

All Matter is Energy

Let's define the word energy. According to the Merriam-Webster dictionary, "energy is the ability to be active: the physical or mental strength that allows you to do things: natural enthusiasm and effort: usable power that comes from heat, electricity, etc."

The term "energy" is the indicator we use to identify and measure our physical and emotional health as well as our physical resources such as oil, electricity and food. We use the word "energy" regularly to describe anything from the gas in our cars, or the electricity in our buildings, to our physical or emotional state. We even have energy bars and energy drinks to help us function at a higher level. We refer to people, places and things as having good or bad energy. In the daily hustle and bustle, "energy," as a word, as a concept, as a fuel, is literally in and around us.

Basic principles of physics tell us all matter is energy. We know energy is something we can never totally get rid of. However, it can be transformed. We burn a piece of paper and it becomes ash; boil water, and it evaporates, becoming water vapor. Energy is a feeling as well. In the spring, most of us experience a heightened sense of euphoria due to the potent force I call energy. This energy is both responsible for, and a result of, the new life emerging from the earth as it resurrects from the deadness of winter. Energy is the key force that creates sustainable power.

Energy is Critical to Our Well-Being

This is true whether we're talking about individuals, families, businesses or countries. When we don't have the resources we need (even if momentarily), we often go into "victim" mode/energy. When we are in a victim state, we feel extremely disempowered and most often are, whether we are broke, jobless, don't have electricity, have been caught up in a tragedy, war, a natural disaster, robbery or illness. It is not until we have the resources we need to take care of ourselves that we begin to feel a sense of survival.

More Energy Equals More Power

Whoever has the oil, whoever has the strongest military, whoever has the most money, the best educational systems (all of which are sources or types of energy) are the countries that have the most authority and domination. These are the countries that wield enormous control and influence. We even rate and label nations based on their resources as first and third world countries.

Because of their lack of resources, third world nations are the least powerful countries in our world, unless of course they are sitting on oil and other untapped sources of energy. Even then, if those countries give away those resources or don't know how to utilize those resources themselves, they still won't have much power. Knowing not only how to identify an energy source, but also taking ownership of it and then using it, is what produces power.

When undeveloped countries have undeveloped resources that are discovered by the "powers that be" it is not uncommon for these resources, whether it's the natural beauty of their land, rain forests, diamonds, plants/trees, oil, or water, to be exploited for money and power, regardless of the cost to that culture. Few people profit from this type of model—what our culture now deems "the one percent."

The loss of dividends for most of the people who live in these countries only further contributes to the cycle of poverty and maintenance of the dysfunctional and destructive type of power that we've seen over and over again in a "man's world."

Women Helping Women Around the World

Many women in third world countries are now learning how to create successful businesses and transform their lives with micro loans and other types of assistance. These women, and men as well, are now able to gain entrepreneurial experience and are given many more opportunities because of organizations like *Kiva* and *Women for Women*.

When my niece was a freshman in college, she used Kiva.org for a school project and loaned $25 dollars to a woman in Africa who owned her own store. While $25 may not be a lot to many of us, this is an example of an evolved new generation of a feminine model of empowerment. Kiva's mission is "to connect people through lending to alleviate poverty." (One of the co-founders is Jessica Jackley. Google her, and I think you'll agree she has one of the most impressive backgrounds I've ever seen.)

Both those giving assistance, as well as the recipients, are inspiring. Together they are creating new ways of controlling their lives and investing in the future of women who previously were victims to their lives. This kind of program is inventive and ingenious. They have developed new models of business, helping to create and promote prosperity and empowerment. You can learn more about Kiva on their website: www.kiva.com.

Women for Women is an international organization that that assists women survivors of war-torn countries. They provide a year-long training program to give these women the tools and skills to support their families and help empower them emotionally. You can find out more about them and their mission at their website: www.womenforwomen.org.

Save the Children (their website: www.savethechildren.org) is another organization that has focused a great deal of its resources toward women and children. For years the director of Save the Children Afghanistan made sure the focus of her program was providing books and schools for girls, as girls were not allowed to go to school there under the reign of the Taliban.

These women are now identifying, owning and utilizing their power in new and inventive ways, creating models for developing economic growth and stabilization for their communities. This is their "way out" of depending on the traditional generosity of the first world. The traditional model rarely impacts the cycles of injustice, violence and poverty. These women have now learned how to use both the outer and inner resources available to them.

As a result, they have been—and still are—developing and implementing new game plans.

These new and sustainable methods are proving to have the power and means needed to make the changes necessary to enable the healthy, safe and stable lives that they and their communities deserve. This creates not only a stable economy, but also an amazing life force that permeates their lives and those around them. They are no longer victims, living in victim energy, but thrivers who now have the confidence, strength, vitality and energy of empowered adults.

Energy Is Our Most Powerful Resource

Defining energy on a personal level means various things, like whether or not we have the "mojo" needed to get out of bed in the morning, are able to be productive throughout the day, see projects through to completion, play with the kids after coming home from work, or feel like making love before we go to sleep. All of these behaviors depend on the amount of the energy we have. Energy is our most powerful resource.

I believe that becoming conscious of our energy as our spirit, and seeing our bodies as a container for that spirit, changes how we feel about ourselves, enabling us to have a more authentic sense of power.

As we will discuss in the next chapter, it is also a bonding force for us in our relationships with others. Becoming aware of using our energy to feel empowered is something I found out about in a very unique way.

Love and the IRS Auditor

Early in my private practice, the IRS audited me. Dealing with numbers, money and the business part of my work has never been a strength of mine, to say the least. As you might imagine, I felt overwhelmed with anxiety and the amount of work needed to organize myself for the audit. Even though my wonderful accountant assured me I had nothing to worry about, I was still terrified.

So I did what I do when faced with a frightening situation. I began to meditate and pray about it.

The day of the audit, a very nerdy and grumpy middle-aged man showed up at my house. Within minutes, it was clear to me that he had most likely been tormented as a child in school, and now he was finally in the threatening position of exacting payback through his power as an auditor.

Even with all of this man's insecurities being so obvious to me, I found myself aggravated by his pickiness and menacing attitude. He appeared to be an extremely unhappy man, and his negative energy filled and polluted my dining room. This was not helping my anxiety level.

Fortunately, my head took over and reminded me that I needed to see this situation from a new perspective. I began to realize that I most likely was right about him, that he probably did have something in his background that made him so unpleasant.

I recalled something I'd read from a class I'd taken through Unity Church. We can look at people from either a place of love or from a place of fear. When we look at people who are difficult or threatening as people who are probably afraid, we see them from a perspective of love. As I recalled this wisdom, I began to imagine white light of unconditional love emanating from my heart toward him.

At this point I wasn't "feeling the love," but I was able to direct my thoughts in a more positive and compassionate way, rather than dwell on my discomfort. Much to my surprise, within five minutes of doing this, the auditor looked up at me and said that he knew he'd been very picky throughout most of the audit. His demeanor changed and he suddenly seemed much nicer, and completed the audit.

The Power of the Heart

After he left, I realized that this audit had happened for a reason. It was the first time I consciously owned the power of thought and energy combined: the power of my heart. This was the beginning of my knowingly utilizing my Feminine Heart Energy! For me it proved to be a great awakening.

This approach has continuously produced amazing results for others as well. This ability to utilize Feminine Heart Energy is essential to achieving higher consciousness. Consciousness is about being awake. Higher consciousness is about being awake beyond the norm. There are people whose perspective has a sense of knowing that is extraordinary; these are the people we tend to view as having wisdom, or you might say, higher consciousness. Their comprehension of life comes from a place of awakening deep within their soul, regardless of their age or circumstances. These are the people who are often referred to as old souls. And these are the people who have Feminine Heart Energy down to their core.

Awaken Your Soul and Express Wisdom in the World

When we intentionally and consciously send our heart energy out into the world, we are, in religious terms, praying. Whatever you want to call it, putting this energy out from our hearts is a way we may awaken our souls and express our wisdom.

Here's an exercise for whenever you have to talk about something difficult to someone. First, take a couple of deep breaths into your heart and imagine your heart filled with white light, and then picture this person/situation. Now form a mental image of speaking from your heart directly and honestly, sending this white light to the recipient. And most importantly, *pray for them to receive what you are saying from the intention from which it is coming.*

My experience is that most times, people will respond positively to whatever you've expressed, or if they don't, you will be fine with accepting their reaction. This technique helps you disconnect (get unhooked) energetically from conflict or defensiveness. It is a great way to learn how to harness your energy and experience authentic "letting go." This is what having Feminine Heart Energy is all about!

Reflections:

1. *What types of food, places and activities, help you feel energized or revitalized? What types of food, places and activities leave you feeling drained and tired?*

2. *If you were able to experience your body as the container for your spirit, how might that impact how you feel about your body?*

3. *Imagine sending heart energy to someone you have conflict with and notice how your body feels.*

4. *Have you ever had the experience of seeing a situation from a new perspective? How did this impact you?*

5. *Take a minute to close your eyes. Take a few deep, slow breaths and bring your awareness to your heart. Imagine that there is an energy that emanates from your heart that flows through your chest and shoulders down through your arms and into your hands. Put the tips of your thumbs and forefingers together.*

   Now imagine that this is a continual flow from your heart that keeps circulating up into your heart and back down again. Picture an ongoing flow of energy coming from within your heart.

   See if you can feel the energy in your body as you use your mind to imagine it. Take a moment to go back to your heart, the source of this energy, and intentionally picture sending that energy out from your heart into the world. Imagine that it is a healing, loving energy that can bless whomever you wish to send it to.

   Continually check in with your body and observe how the physical sensations feel as you do so. See if you can do this without judging yourself or wondering if you are doing it "right." There is no right.

   The goal of this exercise is to help you begin connecting more fully with your heart and feel its energy. If it feels right for you, imagine that your heart is the home for your soul and it is your spirit that you are sending out into the universe.

   For some, this may seem hokey or untenable. Even if you are unable to do this right now, hang in there and just give it a try it daily. Like working out, it may take time to develop this tool for expressing your beautiful feminine loving energy out in the world. Be patient and know that you are contributing in a small but big way to the healing of our planet.

   The next time you hear the sirens of a police car, fire truck or ambulance, send energy of love, light and healing from your heart to everyone involved in whatever is going on, from the first responders to the people needing their assistance. Then pay attention to how it feels to have taken a moment to do so. This is a beautiful way of praying.

Chapter 7

Bonding and Belonging: Home Court Advantage

Relationships are the primary source of energy, and that's what makes the world go round for us personally, professionally and globally. *Relationships help us feel like we matter in life.* The place we most give and receive energy is in our relationships. This chapter is about how powerfully energy bonds and sustains us.

Many universities are known for their legendary football teams as well as their academics. Despite my dislike of violence, I love football and loved going to games when I was in college. I still enjoy going to a game once a year to reconnect with old friends and feel the excitement of campus on a game day. Truth be told, I'm not very invested in who wins. So, I'm not writing about this football phenomenon from the perspective of a rabid fan, but to demonstrate the concept of energy as it contributes to power.

Even if you couldn't care less about (or even hate) sports, the following discussion about college football is meant to help you understand the concept of how energy relates to bonding and power in a very tangible way (not to mention you'll understand why sports is a HUGE moneymaker).

On almost any given fall Saturday on campuses across the country, there is an energy that fans feel from the minute they step on the grounds. This energy feels incredibly alive and special. There are rituals that help create and facilitate energy, bonding and belonging. These include tailgates, pep rallies, music, fight songs, marching bands, college logos and colors that adorn clothing such as tee shirts, sweatshirts and hats. All of which contribute to feeling an affiliation with other fans as well as the institution itself. Then there's the pre-game, half-time, and post-game analysis on television with fans watching from home and at bars. Not to mention the game itself!

Over the years I have been struck by the emotional energy people share for certain universities, both the love *and* intense dislike. People who feel a bond to these schools have relationships with the institution for various reasons: as alumni, family, friend, religious and geographic affiliations.

Many of these people feel such a passionate connection that it often borders on the fanatic. It's fascinating to see such a powerful sense of community and devotion revolving around a college football team. When you think about it from the perspective of bonding and belonging it makes sense that despite even dismal seasons, these institutions of higher learning are still capable of maintaining a powerful vitality and spiritedness for generations. Energy is incredibly bonding, and people tend to return to places, people, and situations that help make them feel alive.

The Real Meaning of Home Court Advantage

In fact, athletic events in general provide a terrific opportunity for me to demonstrate further this concept of energy. *One of the major reasons sports plays such a big role in our society comes from our need to access the life force, or energy, that we're identifying in this chapter.*

When a team does well, it energizes the spectators, whether at the live event or on TV. The opposite is also true: When the fans get excited, the team gets a boost and feeds off the energy of the crowd. Home court advantage is a cultural term meaning the "home" team has a better chance of winning because the home team's fans will be there cheering them on. Being able to tap into and command this energy is what generates the power to win not only ball games, but also elections, the craps table in Vegas, and even wars.

The Zen Master and Energy

Phil Jackson was the head coach of the Chicago Bulls basketball team while Michael Jordan was in his prime. He helped establish the Bulls as a formidable basketball dynasty by winning six NBA championships.

Phil was a unique coach in that for the most part, he didn't tend to scream, yell or behave like a lunatic during games. Often he sat on the sidelines looking calm in the midst of his team's struggles on the court. The press referred to him as the "Zen master."

Phil is a Buddhist. Other coaches and the media often made fun of him for requiring his players to do yoga before it was the "in" thing to do. Phil has been open about his spiritual practices, including using meditation techniques and Native American rituals to help him feel grounded. He wrote a fascinating book titled *Sacred Hoops* that uses basketball as a metaphor for life.

What I respect most about Coach Jackson is his mastery of energy— the source of his success as an NBA coach. His skill at understanding how to utilize and command energy is incredible. He "knew" when it was time to substitute players or call a time out.

Over and over again, Phil Jackson illustrated his wisdom regarding the use of energy and tapped into it during his coaching through championship years with the Chicago Bulls. His coaching is a great example of the unseen yet powerful energy that surrounds and dwells within us.

Bonding and Belonging

At any level, sports provide a way for people to bond and feel a sense of belonging within their communities. Another demonstration of this is the highly rated network television show *Friday Night Lights*. This weekly series told stories about a town in Texas and its local high school football team, families, friends and fans. The show is a clear example of the way in which the culture of a town is organized around its sports teams.

Athletics have become a primary way in which men in particular and schools, towns, cities, and countries form powerful relationships that last generations. Whenever any of the major professional sports teams in my hometown are involved in championship or "big" games, I am struck by the ease with which strangers excitedly talk to one another about it. It's a wonderful an opportunity for us big city dwellers to connect with one another and engage in passionate conversation.

Numerous times, I've witnessed this occurrence on buses, trains, elevators, restaurants, churches and more. Instead of sitting down next to someone, looking straight ahead and ignoring them, it's, "Hey, did you hear if the this team or that team won?" "Sure did. What a game!" It's energy like this that enables us to bond, at least momentarily, and cross the invisible lines that normally keep us distanced. No wonder Michael Jordan was so revered during the height of his success as a professional basketball player!

Another fascinating aspect of sports is the way it provides a means for men in our society to feel comfortable expressing their feelings and bond emotionally with each other. Regardless of whether he is the player or spectator, this is an arena in which the most macho man can demonstrate physical affection with another man, like hugs, pats on the rear end, walking with arms around each others' shoulders, and verbally expressing joy, sadness, friendship and love in front of crowds of people, and very often on camera!

Energy in our culture enables not only strangers in big cities to talk to one another, but men to behave in these affectionate ways towards each other that are extraordinary. As women, we often verbally express our feelings and behave in physically affectionate ways on a regular basis, but for men, there are far fewer socially acceptable outlets for this emotional engagement.

No wonder so many men are so addicted to sports!

Reflections:

1. What types of organizations, people and places give you a sense of belonging and community? Reflect on what the energy feels like in these situations and then observe how your body feels as you do so.
2. How much of your time is spent with these people and in these places? Create a pie chart of your time and activities and note if you are spending enough time in this type of energy.
3. Does this chapter help you understand the role that energy plays in our society as related to feeling a sense of belonging?
4. What other actives besides sports give you a sense of belonging?

SECTION 2

Owning

Chapter 8

The Nose Knows

My friend Alyce and I were having dinner recently when she asked me, "How does someone get in touch with the Feminine Heart Energy you talk about in your book?" Good question.

Unlike Mary the Blessed Mother, I did not have an angel appear with a message, but I do recall sitting in my office listening to a client and suddenly feeling like I had champagne bubbles dancing on the tip of my nose.

I was a relatively new therapist, but some part of me "knew" that this was an indicator for me to say something that, quite frankly, seemed totally unrelated to what my client was talking about. As the sensation intensified, I decided to trust my nose and say what I was feeling compelled to say. I opened my mouth, let it fly, and the words that came out of my mouth were perfect.

My client had arrived this day looking stressed and sad. As he began discussing his challenging relationship with his wife, I found myself thinking that I should ask him if there was something going on with one of his friends. I kept telling myself that this had nothing to do with his marriage. So why did I keep thinking about this? The intensity of my nose bubbles heightened as these thoughts increased. They began to distract me from listening to him.

I finally spoke up and told him that for some reason, I kept having the thought that I should ask him about a friend? He looked astonished and burst into tears. He told me he had just found out that a very good friend of his was very sick and most likely he was going to die soon. He acknowledged that he was distraught about this even though they hadn't seen each other very often in the last couple of years.

The course of our session changed and it was clear that *this* was the issue he needed to talk about. When he left he thanked me, and he looked a heck of a lot better than when he arrived. This was the first time I realized my nose could sniff out more than just smells!

From that day on, every time my nose has that champagne bubble sensation, I trusted whatever I said or did would be exactly what was needed, even if I couldn't immediately recognize its sense of relevance to the situation. It works like magic. I've even had clients who asked me if I am psychic (I'm not). For those first few years, believe it or not, my nose was my divining rod. I owned my power the day I decided to trust what I now recognize as an indicator of my Feminine Heart Energy.

No More Bubbles

Years later, while teaching a class of graduate students, I shared the story about my nose bubbles, and while doing so I realized that it had been several years since I'd had that sensation. I had gotten so used to trusting my intuition, the external signal was no longer necessary. After years of training, experience, and nose bubbles, I had developed a level of competence and confidence that was very empowering. I felt consistently directed by my Feminine Heart Energy, my God voice within, my inner "knowing."

Whatever name you want to call it, this energy has been and is still what assists me most in my work. Much like my nose bubbles, you too have your own guiding indicators, and listening to your body is the doorway that accesses your Feminine Heart Energy.

As the old saying goes, we teach what we need to learn. I also believe we learn what we need to teach. As a new therapist, I was eager to continue my postgraduate training. Part of that for me was resuming my own therapy in the early 80s. I found a wonderful therapist who was "body-centered" in his approach. This was different from anything I'd ever encountered in graduate school, and later on realized that this method of therapy was way ahead of its time.

As a result of my personal experience, I pursued training in this area of study and eventually it became the cornerstone of my approach to treatment. To say I can't imagine how I would even begin to work with clients without this body-centric knowledge is an understatement.

Let me tell you why: The focus of this type of treatment is using the physical sensations in the body to identify emotional feelings. As adults we tend to be in our heads a great deal. We've got to change that so we can tap into the physical signs of our Feminine Heart Energy.

Thoughts, Feelings and Change

We've spent the previous part of the chapter looking at how I have utilized my body to access and develop my intuition. It's only fair that our beautiful brains get airtime as well!

It is a commonly held understanding that the way we think is critical to the way we experience life. This is clearly demonstrated by the cliché question, "Is the glass half full or half empty?" One of the great things about our thoughts is that they are relatively easy to change. There are schools of thought that maintain that how we think is the "be all and end all" when it comes to our mental health or spiritual well-being.

As a psychotherapist, I believe that how we think has an important effect on how we feel. However, I also believe that *JUST changing our thought process is not always enough in order to effect change.* It has been my experience that, in order for real change to occur, you must also learn to:

- Download new tools and skills.
- Release emotions in healthy, appropriate ways.
- Allow time for these new behavioral patterns to really take root (this is why the length of treatment programs for trauma and addiction tends to be 21 to 28 days).

The place where most people begin to effect any kind of change is thinking differently. In the language of psychotherapy this is known as cognitive restructuring. Change is virtually impossible without it.

Speaking of change, this book is consistently inviting you to think about how YOU think about yourself, being a woman, and your value in the world.

I believe there will be incredible shifts in consciousness not only for yourself as an individual, but for society as a whole, when we women see ourselves as beautiful vessels of divine light and love.

Back to The Body

If you observe children, you'll likely notice they are much more in their bodies than we adults are. I believe our heads and thoughts are very important components of life's discernments, however, when we really listen to the body, we will experience a deeper truth. This is because we are NOT able to justify, rationalize and minimize our thoughts.

As critical thinkers, we are taught to judge our feelings and thoughts, but our bodies do not naturally make such judgments. There is no judgment or critical evaluation within the body, only sensations. Each of us has internal wiring via our physical sensations that communicates important and sometimes critical information. Whether we listen to it or not is another story.

My friend Alyce the author of *Gut Wisdom*, the same one who asked me the question about Feminine Heart Energy, has been a healthcare provider for over 20 years. She helps her clients identify the correlation between emotional well-being and physical health. Considering our bodies are the housing for our souls, it makes sense that they have an innate wisdom.

The Body Doesn't Lie

Helping clients listen to their bodies enables them to connect/reconnect to their true selves. The body does not lie. For example, a sick feeling in the stomach and a cold feeling all over for no apparent reason are often indicators of fear. Many people can identify this pretty universal sensation.

There is a good reason these sensations occur: If we don't pay attention to these body sensations, which have been put place to guide us, we will frequently experience emotional and/or physical dis-ease.

Often, upon looking back, most people recognize that their regrets in life stem from having disregarded their own bodily signals and sensations.

When beginning work with a new client, I often need to teach them how to ground themselves in their bodies.

Grounding yourself is essential in order to help you become more tuned into your feelings, intuition and wisdom. If you are not grounded in your body when intense feelings arise (especially anxiety), you will experience being overwhelmed or flooded by them. So it is really important that we are regularly centered in our bodies. Here are a few simple techniques I use and that my clients have found to be successful:

1. **BREATHE.** Put your feet flat on the floor, close your eyes, then BREATHE! When you breathe, make sure you are breathing into your belly. It can be very useful to take a deep breath into the belly, filling it up, bringing the air into your upper chest and then picture that you can bring it all the way into the tips of your shoulders. Hold your breath and very slowly count to four before releasing, then exhale. When exhaling, make sure you control your breath in a slow and steady manner. This particular breathing technique is really helpful in calming the body quickly. Do as many breaths as needed. I find that most people need at least six in order to feel relaxed and more connected to their body.

2. **WALK.** If you can, walk along a beach in sand with your shoes off, especially in cooler weather. Pay attention to how your feet feel with the sand between your toes. Notice the rest of your body. Observe. You will most likely feel your energy feel as if it is being pulled downwards into the sand. Find a big tree nearby (an oak tree is especially good) and sit with your back against it for 10 minutes. Breathe into your tailbone; imagine connecting your breath to the roots of the tree. The effect from this is as good as 30

or more minutes of meditation; again your energy should feel a downward pull. Go for a walk or hike somewhere in nature and notice your energy and how soothing it feels.

3. NOTICE. Sitting with your feet flat, breathe into your belly a few times to get settled. Then bring your awareness to your feet. Notice your heels, instep, toes and every other part of your feet. Notice if your feet feel heavy and what their temperature is like. Then bring your awareness to your legs and once again, observe them piece by piece. Feel the hamstrings and then the shin bones and then the knees. Go from there to the back of the thighs, then the top of your thighs.

Continue exploring all of your body parts without judging or trying to change how they feel. Just observe without judgment, and notice how it feels as you go further up your body. How is your breathing? How does your stomach feel, is it hungry, empty, relaxed? How does your neck feel, is it tight or relaxed? How about your shoulders, arms, wrists, hands, fingers and fingernails? As you continue focusing on your body and its physical sensations, you will feel calmer because you are more connected to it. When you are connected with your body, you will be grounded in it, and that's when you will feel safe and secure internally.

4. IMAGINE. A guided imagery that can be very useful (and yes, you need to begin this first with deep breathing) is to imagine your body as a tree. Picture your lower part (from the waist down) as the trunk of the tree, and your upper body as the branches of the tree, reaching into the sky. As you breath deep into your belly, picture your breath going down through the lower part of your body (the imagine your body legs and through your feet as though your breath was able to take root into the earth. With each breath, see the roots getting stronger and deeper into the dirt, going through the minerals, clay, and rocks to the center to connect at the core of Mother Earth.

Let yourself imagine that the power in this core is regenerative, peaceful, warm and loving...like the ideal mother. Now picture that the roots you've put down there are able to pull this Mother Earth energy right up into your feet, up through your legs and into the rest of your body. As you do this, feel the physical sensations, notice your breathing, and just observe how calm and relaxed and yet strong your body feels.

These are just a few exercises to assist you in feeling solid and grounded in your body. Like trees, we need to have strong inner roots in order to withstand wind and storms. Being grounded is perhaps the most important inner resource we have. Without it we are unable to connect with our higher and true selves.

Dissociation, Depression, Anxiety and the Body

People who come from highly dysfunctional and especially abusive families tend to "leave" their bodies at an early age as a means of emotional survival. The psychological term for this is dissociation. So great is the anxiety due to their physical and spiritual disconnect, they are unable to mine the wealth of information that exists within their own bodies to decide what is right for them in any given moment. It's almost impossible to own your power when this is going on. Dissociation is common (even if temporarily) for people who have had any type of trauma.

Depression and/or anxiety are the normal emotional aftermath that occurs when we experience a situation that accounts for feeling depressed or anxious. Examples of this are death, divorce, and loss of a job. Whereas when one has what we call a *biological depression or anxiety disorder*, there may or may not be a situation that triggers these feelings.

Anxiety and depressive disorders can block the body's ability to communicate effectively with the self. If while walking down a street you begin to feel your heart palpitate, feel like you can't breathe, begin to perspire, have obsessive compulsive thoughts or are overwhelmed by feeling out of control, it is nearly impossible to be able to evaluate what is going on. Our bodies are built to be able to "know" whether we need to get off that street and take another route; or go to the hospital and get checked out.

When someone has an anxiety disorder their "knowing" is interrupted. They are emotionally and physically disabled. Often this disorder manifests in obsessive-compulsive thoughts, feelings and behavior. Some common symptoms are an inability to trust that they locked the door, and feeling uncertain, needing to check it again and again. Other examples include phobias; even when effected people intellectually know and remind themselves over and over that most elevators are safe, or that they are far more likely to be in a car accident than a plane crash, they still can feel paralyzed and unable to fly or to get on an elevator without being terrified.

Imagine knowing your material for a work presentation inside and out, and in spite of taking many deep breaths to help release the tension, you are overwhelmed with fear and panic in the moment you're presenting. Similarly, when a person is depressed, the symptoms of low energy, lack of interest in activities that you would normally enjoy, lack of (or too much) sleep, no appetite or overeating, lack of libido, feeling sad and thinking despairing thoughts, or lack of concentration or ability to make decisions certainly impact our ability to have a clear and accurate connection to ourselves, which leaves us feeling powerless. These symptoms all limit our ability to connect to our bodily sensations.

Addictions

In addition to depression and anxiety being impairments to connecting to your true self, so are other things such as addictions.

The irony with addiction is that the only way to recover is to learn how to connect with your true self, rather than the addictive self. However, the addict needs to get free from drugs and alcohol in order to do so. While someone is using or is in the early stage of recovery, it is impossible for them to think clearly as an addiction is, by its nature, something that distorts one's thinking process. That's one of the reasons Alcoholics Anonymous can be so useful, as the 12 steps provide the tools and skills to assist in members learning to think and behave in new and healthy ways, which then assists addicts in getting to know their true selves.

Paying Attention to People, Places and Things

It is also critical to be mindful of how situations or relationships we are involved in can impact us negatively. This includes being around people who are toxic to us. They could be family members, or a spouse, or a friend who is very critical or negative, or a boss who is tyrannical. It can also be when we react to toxic people or conditions in inappropriate or abusive ways.

We likewise interrupt our connection to our true self when we view too much television, indulge in indiscriminate sex, watch violent movies, read too many mindless books and magazines that are like junk food for the brain, feed our body literal junk food, gossip, overspend, and mindlessly shop and buy items to fill a void.

We humans all have experienced things that we "know" impact us in unhealthy and negative ways when we engage in too much of whatever it is. Health is about having balance and boundaries!

When we are in balance and have good boundaries we are not held hostage by these disorders, addictions, or unhealthy people, situations, or patterns of behavior... and then we are free to have a clear connection to our core self through our body.

Whether deciding if we should stay in relationships, take certain jobs, change our diet, go to the doctor, have a baby, buy a house, or even something as simple as avoiding certain traffic routes, our bodies can and will guide us to decisions that will be for our highest good if we are willing to learn to pay attention to them. As we discussed in an earlier chapter, follow the energy and you will "know" what is right for you in any given situation.

Notice if a church, home, restaurant or other space feels good and boosts your energy just walking in the door. When we are in circumstances in which we feel energized we feel it in our body, this then feeds our body, mind and soul.

Do Right by Your Soul

We need to look within our bodies for our own wisdom. The body is, after all, the temple of the soul, the spirit and the heart. I believe that our Feminine Heart Energy is our spirit. We cannot get to our innate store of wisdom without first going through the body. So, if we learn to connect to our internal body sensations, we will have access to the answers we seek.

You may be familiar with the commercial featuring a man walking all over the world with his cell phone, asking the question, "Can you hear me now?" Sometimes our connection to ourselves is like our cell phone providers: Some are better than others; some work well in some areas, but not in others; with some there's often static or dropped calls. Depending on your needs, you have to decide what service is best for you.

This is not any different than our "connection" to our selves. We need to assess if we have the right carrier, the means, to make sure we are able to "hear" ourselves consistently.

If you don't already know your access points to connect with your body, mind and soul, explore various pathways using the exercises earlier in this chapter. Then your job is to follow the energy and find rituals that can assist you in maintaining a great connection to yourself.

If you already know what your access points to your spirit are, then make sure you check in on a regular basis. If you're not doing whatever it is you know is right for your soul, and aren't able to get back on track, look for and get the support you need to help you. Take care of yourself. You deserve it!!

Finding the Pathway to Yourself

Here are some practices that can assist you in connecting and strengthening your bond with your inner self:

- – Meditation
- – Exercise
- – Art
- – Music
- – Nature

- Writing
- Dance
- Pursuing hobbies you enjoy
- Cook
- Volunteer
- Sing
- Spend time with people/animals you love
- Take a class that stretches you beyond your comfort level

These are activities that can help you gain access to Feminine Heart Energy. These pursuits can help you feel alive and create a sense of well-being. Creativity and self-care are often direct routes to the life force within ourselves. They can provide us with a pathway to the parts of ourselves that help heal and guide us.

Talk about an information highway! This is why meditation is so useful; it's like having Wi-Fi instead of dial-up. When you consistently listen to yourself from this place of a quiet mind, you connect with the deeper parts of yourself, your spirit, intuition, wisdom, the God within, whatever you want to call it.

It's what you experience when you breathe deeply; feel the physical sensations of your body that enable you to feel grounded; how you can feel both peaceful and energized after yoga; when you get a runner's high; when you find yourself moved to tears by the beauty of a symphony; when you can't stop writing even though you are exhausted; when you are so involved in a creative activity that you don't even notice the time passing.

It's also the afterglow following making love, and the magical softening that we feel holding a baby or even petting a puppy or kitten. This is how you will feel when you are being intimate with this deeper feminine beloved part of yourself. When you recognize and embrace these beautiful feelings as part of your power, you are truly in Holy Communion with the human and the divine. And this is when you experience your heart opening fully to express the best part of who you are! Namaste!

Reflections:

1. Do you ever experience your own version of nose bubbles? How does it manifest for you? What happens to you when this happens?
2. How might you treat your body differently if you believed it was the vessel for your spirit?
3. Do you tend to trust your gut? Identify a time you did. What were the consequences as a result? Identify a time you did not. What was the outcome?
4. Are you able to consistently feel a physical connection to your body? Is it easy or challenging for you to feel grounded?
5. If you struggle with anxiety, depression or addiction, has this chapter helped you to better understand how this impairs your ability to experience a true sense of power? If needed, are you willing to get the help you deserve?
6. What are your specific "access points" to connect with your inner self/ spirit?

Chapter 9

When Angels Open Doors, or Faith vs. Fear

There is an old saying: When there is faith there is no fear.

I beg to differ. If there were no fear, then why would we need faith? Faith is when we go forward in spite of our fear. Remember, "the place God calls you is the place where your deep gladness meets the world's deep needs." When you follow your true calling or intuition, whatever it may be at any given time, you will get whatever you need to go there.

Or as I like to say, "when angels open doors." This is an important concept in order for us to really understand an evolved perspective of empowerment.

Trust That There is a Reason For Everything

An updated sense of empowerment is about trusting our hearts and following the energy. This is living an abundance mindset. Living in abundance is about trust, trusting that we are enough and that there will be enough of whatever we need to meet those deep needs. In other words: trusting that there is a reason for everything, especially when we can't see what that reason is at any given time.

I believe this is true because I see people gain new perspectives, or what I like to think of as "miracles," almost every day in my line of work when

71

they are following their hearts. I have experienced this in my own life, too. Here's an example:

My first job out of graduate school, as I mentioned in chapter one, was as an addiction counselor. The following year, I became director of the program.

Working at a treatment center for chemically dependent women was one of the most incredible experiences of my life, but as rewarding as the job could be, it was equally stressful. I was frequently exhausted, and at the age of 28 I was already beginning to feel a sense of burnout. In spite of my love for the place and the incredibly courageous women I counseled there, I knew that I needed a job change, and soon.

One night after an especially challenging day at work, I off-handedly joked to my co-worker, Joan, that I needed a new job. She replied that her roommate Jillian needed a cook for a graduate program she was running in Israel. In that moment, I experienced what felt like a bolt of lightning shooting through my body, and instantly knew I needed to go, even though I had no clue why.

Now, as much as I loved to travel, Israel had never been on my radar screen as a place of interest. I'm not Jewish and, although I was raised Catholic, the whole "Holy Land" thing did nothing for me. Joan and her roommate Jillian, whom I knew and liked, were both Catholic nuns.

I was happy to have dinner every couple of months with these intriguing ladies, but I was also a typical 28-year-old single woman whose attention was focused more on going out with friends and dating than on spending four months living with a group of nuns, priests and seminarians—and in a monastery no less!

The reasons NOT to go to Israel were abundantly clear, and yet I knew it was what I had to do. The man I had hoped to marry had recently met someone else and I was still recovering from major heartbreak. Perhaps that had something to do with my impulse to go to Israel for a semester of study abroad as one of only two cooks. Perhaps not. All I know is, whatever my reasons for going, it was absolutely the right decision. The opportunity changed my life forever.

All the Reasons Not to Go...

Once Jillian told me "it's a go," I contacted my boss, and informed him that I was interested in taking a leave of absence from my position. He told me that because I was the director of the program, he didn't think he could let me go. Spontaneously, I replied, "I'm not asking if you'll let me go; I'm going. I'm asking whether you'll give me a leave or not." I'd never felt so clear about something. The peace I felt as I spoke to him was extraordinary.

I let him know that I would completely understand if he needed to replace me. I knew then and there that expressing what I needed (instead of asking for permission) was the key to the new sense of power I felt at that moment. I trusted that no matter what he decided, I was going to Israel, and all would be well. It was incredibly freeing. Within days, my boss informed me that my job would be waiting for me when I returned in four months.

Coincidences Are A Validation That You're on the Right Path

In the meantime, my two roommates wanted to know how I would be paying my share of the rent on our three-bedroom apartment while I was gone. They weren't the only ones! I might be getting my job back upon my return, but I most certainly wasn't going to be paid while I was gone.

Since my pay (as is common for most social service agencies) was near poverty level, and I was also paying back huge student loans, my financial circumstances were bleak.

Considering this state of affairs, I was strangely calm, taken over by a "knowing" that I was doing the right thing. Intuitively I trusted that somehow it would all work out. As I continued making my plans, I received a phone call from my friend Amy from Boston, who also knew my roommates.

It turned out that Amy needed to be in town for four months in the fall and she was calling to ask if she could camp out on our couch during this time. She was hoping that, rather than have to rent an apartment for such a short period of time; she could live with us and share our expenses. What a "coincidence" that she needed a place to live during the exact time I was to be gone! (By the way, Amy met her husband during the time she lived there, coincidence indeed!) This journey was already proving to be amazing and I hadn't even left yet.

Now, the fun part! My boss called to tell me one of my co-workers was moving and that I was the one he wanted to fill her position. I was ecstatic. I had secretly been lusting for this job—it seemed ideal for me—but it was one I never expected would become available for quite some time. One catch, however: I couldn't go to Israel. I had to start right away.

I prayed about this. I wondered what the hell I was doing, going on a four-month program with nuns and priests, taking scripture classes, living in Israel instead of snapping up my dream job, a job I envisioned would provide me with many years of security!

One thing kept coming clear: I needed to go to Israel no matter what. I began to realize this choice had nothing to do with choosing a job. It had to do with choosing to trust and honor my inner voice, my powerful intuition. I knew this leap of faith was crucial for my spiritual development.

Feeling Like a Kid on Christmas Morning

Now you're probably expecting me to impart that something magical happened while I was in the Holy Land. Well, it did and it didn't. It was a life-changing experience, wonderfully educational, spiritually rewarding, frightening, great fun and eye-opening. I loved my time in Israel. For me, the magic was that I had followed my heart and my heart led me to the power of "knowing." This is how I came to own my Feminine Heart Energy. It was during my trip, in a class on the New Testament, when I heard the statement that radically impacted the way I would think, act and teach for the rest of my life:

A miracle is being able to see the same thing from a new perspective.

What an amazing new perspective that trip afforded me, not only along the way, but even after my return.

As I was preparing to come home from my semester in Israel, I realized I literally had $20 left to my name. Even though I would be returning to my job, I wouldn't be receiving a paycheck for another month. I also realized I didn't even have enough money for a bus pass to get to work. According to my calculations, I would need at the very least $200 to survive until I got paid.

At that time, my parents were somewhere in the process of supporting the last seven or more of their 10 children as well as paying their Catholic school tuitions, all on a firefighter's salary no less. Needless to say, I wasn't comfortable asking them for even $200. Initially upon recognizing the direness of my financial situation I panicked but, reminding myself that everything had fallen into place so far in order for me to go on this trip, I trusted that somehow things would work out on the other end when I got home.

Upon my arrival at the airport one of the first things my mom said was that she didn't want to forget to give me a piece of mail that came to their house for me. Both she and I remarked how odd it was that I had received mail at their address; it had been several years since I'd lived with my parents.

But, sure enough, sitting on their kitchen counter was the envelope addressed to me. The letter was from my first employer following my college graduation *seven* years previous! Inside the mystery envelope was a letter informing me that they'd recently done an audit and found that I was owed money. Included with the letter was a check—I kid you not—for $250.00. It was perfect! It was even more than the $200 I would need to commute to work and be able to eat for a month. (God even threw in a little fun money!)

I love and savor the memory of the feeling I had when I first saw that check. I felt like a kid on Christmas morning that had gotten exactly what she'd secretly hoped Santa would bring her. It was magical, thrilling, and almost comical. I just shook my head smiling, as though God and I had just shared a great inside joke.

A Source Greater Than Ourselves

I still recall opening that envelope and seeing that check. I remind myself of this extraordinary moment at times when I feel anxious, and it helps me to remember that *whenever I follow my heart, I will be provided for.* This conscious recollection is a tool I use to help me live from a place of faith and abundance.

Often we ignore our inner callings because we don't have the money, time or whatever. I certainly did not have the money to take a semester to go study abroad.

Principles of prosperity teach that when we receive a calling we will always get the resources we need to manifest what we are called to do.

Receiving that check is a terrific example of this principle, and also demonstrates how resources frequently come in unexpected ways from unexpected sources. The most important thing to remember is that ultimately everything (money, time, love, jobs, homes) comes from a Source greater than ourselves.

Our job, as recipients of universal resources, is to listen to the guidance of our inner "God-voice." When we listen to and trust this internal resource, the external resources are always provided for us. In some circles this is called being "in the flow."

No matter what you call it, when we are consciously connected to the God-Voice within, we will be supported and led to where ever we need to be.

Better Than She Could Even Imagine

The converse is that when we are NOT where we need to be, it's usually obvious as well. Not only will we "know" the real truth deep inside ourselves if we're honest, but also because we won't receive the help we need to go where we want to go. The universe continually guides us. It gives us the external resources we need to support our inner voice. If something is for our highest good we will inevitably get what we need to manifest it.

This doesn't happen if it's not for our highest good. Even when we think that we are being guided from our heart, the universe will nudge us away from whatever isn't in our best interest. (Well, sometimes it's more than a nudge!)

When we are living from a place of faith and open to universal guidance, we usually learn that whatever didn't work out the way we thought it should (the job, the house, the man) is because there is something better. And when we let go of the outcome, it's usually far better than we could ever have imagined.

My friend Norine is a great example of this. She was engaged to a man that she found out was cheating on her. As you can imagine, Norine was devastated. She ended the relationship and was sad, lonely and single for several years.

Then she reconnected on Facebook with Bob, an old friend from college who she had not seen for many years. In the meantime he'd been married and divorced, and had two grown children. Long story short, Norine and Bob began dating. They fell madly in love and got married a year later. It is obvious to all who know them that they have an extraordinary connection and are the loves of each other's lives. They even look like a match physically!

Once Norine began dating Bob, she realized it made sense why she went several years without having someone in her life after her engagement was called off. Bob wasn't available during those years. She is also grateful that her ex-fiancé cheated on her because if she'd married him, she would never have known the kind of love she now had with Bob.

There's an Old 12 Step Saying: "You Can't Push the River"

When we try to force things to happen, or we get attached to a particular outcome, we are usually not where we need to be. This is because we aren't in "right" relationship with ourselves or our situation in some way. We will know this because we will be stuck somehow in our lives. Things won't be working well.

For some people this means "hitting bottom" of some sort. For others, it's as simple as not having enough: enough money, time, friends, etc. This is not about God or the angels being punitive or uncaring about our desires. It's the universe's way of trying to get us on track with our purpose.

Every day, I see this happening in the lives of my clients. When we are on track and connecting with our higher self, something happens that I refer to as "Angels opening doors." My situation with the $250 check was not about the money as much as it was about reinforcing that I had done the absolute right thing by following that "knowing," by listening to my "God-voice." I felt like Dorothy in the Wizard of Oz being led down the yellow brick road.

Off to See The Wizard

I came back from my Israel adventure and returned to my life. I went back to my old job and unfortunately, my co-workers did not welcome me with open arms. They were hostile, angry and resentful. I couldn't blame them.

While I was gone, the agency did what most social service agencies would do: They gave all my work to my already overworked colleagues, and (of course) did not compensate them in any way. To put it mildly, they were not happy with me. As much as I understood, it made me acutely aware that I was going to have to get a new job, and soon. Work was awful.

In the meantime, the dream job my boss had offered me prior to going to Israel had been given away to someone named Patricia. She and I became great friends as well as colleagues. (We never would have met if I had taken the job instead of going to Israel.) And as it turned out, Patricia quit the job several months following my return to go into private practice. My boss called and again offered me the position. This time I took it.

Soon it became apparent that it was also time for me to go into private practice. It was my very good friend Patricia who encouraged and counseled me in this huge step. She was on my speed dial anytime I was scared, telling me I was going to be fine. To this day, we continue to support each other both professionally and personally. She is a life-long friend. Talk about receiving a resource from an unexpected place!

The more I look back, the more I see I was being led to exactly the right people, places and things that would enable me to do the work I was meant to do. Once again, angels were opening doors. It was the first time I became conscious that I had the power to choose to live from a place of faith instead of fear.

So what does any of this have to do with Feminine Heart Energy? It has everything to do with it. Although years ago, I hadn't yet conceived of the concept of Feminine Heart Energy, my whole journey was about trusting my heart to guide me. I followed my calling, and was guided and given all the external resources I needed to get where I needed to go. The universe supported me in this journey of blind faith.

My faith and trust in my intuition and my God-voice was solidified. And this enabled me not only to go to Israel, but also to change the course of my career, and with great fear but even more faith, begin my private practice as a psychotherapist.

Reflections:

1. Can you recall a time when "angels opened doors for you" and things just fell into place? If so, do you remind yourself of this experience when you are lacking faith?

2. What do you imagine your life would be like if you were able to consistently live from a place of faith instead of fear?

3. How does seeing something from a new perspective enable you to experience abundance in your life?

Chapter 10

Love, Lemonade and Miracles— From Surviving to Thriving

In the 80s, I attended a talk Bernie Siegel, MD, gave in Chicago about his groundbreaking book *Love, Medicine and Miracles*. As a prominent surgeon in oncology, he observed behavior patterns that were shared by the many patients he treated over the years. He stated that although he had witnessed many miracles throughout this time, a "miracle" didn't necessarily mean the patient lived.

Dr. Siegel said healing is not about whether we live or die. It is about the transformation that can occur when, as a result of facing a life-threatening illness, people connect with their hearts and souls. For some, it might be the first time in their lives they tell a family member that they love them. Or it might be that the last few months spent with loved ones are filled with more quality time than in all the years previous.

When The World As We Know It Falls Apart

Personal transformation often happens as a result of situations we initially see as awful problems. Life's challenges and traumas can be prime catalysts for transformation. Most people are unable to see from a new perspective without first going through the process of transformation. *Transformation usually occurs when there is a time in our lives when the world as we know it falls apart.*

Transformation is about waking up. Some people resist change as if their lives depend on it. And they are right; our lives DO depend on our ability to change. If we are not able or willing to go through a process of change and give up the old ways of being, we will stay stuck, and often die, emotionally and literally.

Transformation is about a shift in perception. It is seeing the bad stuff as opportunities. If someone has a life-threatening illness, it is an opportunity to change. People who have suffered catastrophic challenges are often afterwards able to express gratitude about the changes they've experienced as a result. Crisis is something that frequently inspires people to move into their hearts.

When bad things happen, these are opportunities to create pathways to opening our hearts and minds to new ways of being, ways that usually bring us to a place of insight. Ways that facilitate strength, wisdom and Higher Consciousness. When you are able to start asking yourself, "What can I learn from this challenge?" and, "How can I grow from this situation?" you are then living in a place of higher consciousness and you are able to transform yourself.

Elizabeth's Story

Elizabeth is a successful architect. She is also a courageous woman, a woman who learned to open her heart. At the time I met her she was a workaholic and her identity was defined by her career.

Elizabeth came to see me for treatment of major depression. She had been sexually and physically abused by her father throughout her childhood. As a result, Elizabeth was loaded with feelings of shame, to say the least. For the first six months of her therapy, she sat on my couch and sobbed. Her shame and grief were palpable.

As you might imagine, her self-esteem was pretty much in the toilet. The day she got married was a nightmare for her, because her role as "The Bride" put her at the center of attention. This was emotionally horrifying for her. Elizabeth knew that her reaction to this was not "normal," and she didn't want to continue allowing the shame she felt from her past to run her life.

Even though we worked on this issue for months before the wedding, she barely got through what should have been one of the happiest days of her life without having a major panic attack.

Fortunately, Elizabeth had been in al-anon at the time she came to see me for treatment of what turned out to be post-traumatic stress disorder. Her time in this group had been fruitful for many reasons.

For one, it gave her the tools and social support system she needed to be able to deal with the abuse issues. As well the 12 steps of the program gave her a spiritual platform which enabled her to begin to experience some hope. It was also during this time that she met her husband, a good, kind, respectful soul who was very patient throughout her struggles with severe depression that medicine helped only minimally.

In addition to attending al-anon meetings, Elizabeth worked diligently and bravely with me in my office. Once she began to deal with her history of abuse, she went to the deepest part of her woundedness and came out stronger and more whole than she could have ever imagined. She began to feel "normal." Elizabeth no longer felt like an impostor; she reported feeling more congruent in how she experienced her internal reactions to situations, and with how she appeared externally to others. She was no longer filled with the shame and fear that accompanies the torment and abuse she experienced as a child.

What she knew in her head about the abuse (that none of it was her fault, that it didn't define who she was, that it didn't mean there was something wrong with her just because something wrong happened to her) was now information that she had downloaded into her body and soul as well. Elizabeth was able not only to see herself and her history from a new perspective, but also to open her heart and love the child part of herself that was incredibly strong and often quite ingenious in her ability to survive a seriously damaging and dysfunctional family situation.

Elizabeth began to love herself and feel whole for the first time in her life. From the moment she walked in my office, I thought she was one of the kindest and caring people I'd met. How wonderful that she was beginning to see herself as who she truly is: a beautiful, heart-centered woman who happens to be an architect! We joyfully ended her treatment after a couple of years of working together.

About six months later I got a phone message from Elizabeth telling me she had had a miscarriage and needed to see me for a session. Quite honestly, I was very concerned about how this heartbreak might affect her. I was afraid she might plunge back into another bout of serious depression. We scheduled an appointment immediately.

Elizabeth sat on my couch and indeed looked sad. "I am very sad," she told me, "That's why I'm here. But I also want to tell you that I am very clear about why I had this miscarriage. As you know, we have been unsuccessfully trying to get pregnant for some time now. So when I finally did conceive, I was thrilled and afraid at the same time. I was concerned that if I lost this baby I would get severely depressed like I was before I got better. Now I know why I had the miscarriage. I believe it was God's way of letting me see how healthy I am. Like I said, I am very sad, but it's appropriate sadness, it's not 'trauma.' I'm sad just like any woman would be from having a miscarriage."

She sat up and continued, "I know that if this had happened before I had therapy, I would have been suicidal. Now, I'm not even close to that, I'm just grieving. So, as difficult as this has been, I see that I am truly better. Now I'm just like anyone dealing with whatever life hands her; I'm no longer a raw wound."

From Surviving to Thriving

What a great example of a person who has gone from being a victim to survivor to thriver! As a thriver, Elizabeth is now truly able to own her power. In her therapy she learned to see her life's challenges from a new perspective. In other words: She made a miracle.

By getting help, she took responsibility for doing the hard work necessary to heal the injured parts of herself. As you can imagine given her history, the biggest challenge and healing she had was being able to connect with and open her wounded heart.

With hard work and the support system of a loving husband and wonderful friends she was able to heal and grow. And, as a result, she was most importantly able to forgive herself, as well as her perpetrator. Elizabeth was even able to view him and the abuse that happened to her from a new perspective. This is the process by which she came into her strength and felt and new sense of heart-centered power.

Elizabeth's story exemplifies how transformation can be, and often is, the doorway to a new way of owning power. It is what occurs when someone takes lemons and makes lemonade!

Change is Not Easy

As most of us know, change is not easy. Elizabeth knew she needed to get help with her depression because it was affecting her job performance, and this meant she was going to have to make some changes. She knew she was going to have to be willing to talk about things she'd not been able to face before.

Her previous approach had been to keep her feelings in and not let anyone know how horrible she felt inside. She had become a good actress around her co-workers, friends and family. When her feelings finally began to overwhelm her and she was having a hard time containing them she did reach out for help. So for her, getting into therapy was the shift she made. Because of her hard work she was able to see her miscarriage as a growthful opportunity.

There are many things (usually external factors) that challenge the status quo of our lives as we know them and create a "shift." The following conceptualization helps explain the process we go through when we change. This was taught to me by my mentor Jane Gerber. It was conceived by renowned and beloved teacher, author and therapist Virginia Satir. It's called the "Satir Change Model" from the book The Satir Model: Family Therapy and Beyond. I love this conceptualization, and have used it countless times over the years as a teaching tool in my practice and consulting work. I think it is very helpful and often reassuring (especially the "chaos" stage) in understanding how change works, and why sometimes it doesn't.

For each stage of change, I have included two examples to help explain the concept. The first example (A) is about someone having an alcohol problem and the second (B) is about someone going through a divorce. Whether it be good or bad, anything else that is about a change in life (like getting sick, fired, married, new job) fits this model as well.

The Stages of Change:

1. STATUS QUO— This is what's familiar, though not necessarily comfortable.

A. For example, waking up regularly with a hangover is not comfortable, nor is waking up and not knowing what you did the night before, but these things are experiences that are often familiar to someone with an alcohol problem.

B. Living in an unhappy or dysfunctional or abusive marriage where you feel sad, angry, miserable or scared most of the time is not comfortable, but it is familiar.

2. FOREIGN ELEMENT— Something happens to shake up the status quo.

A. In the case of someone with a drinking problem, perhaps you get a DUI, or you lose your job, or your family stages an intervention. Sometimes you just get sick and tired of feeling sick and tired.

B. In the case of a divorce you might possibly find out your spouse is cheating on you or you might cheat on your spouse. Or your spouse files for divorce. Or perhaps you take a class that stretches you and enables you to feel stronger and more alive and finally ready to leave. Or maybe you have a significant birthday that makes you reflect on your life in a new way and decide you want more.

3. STATE OF CHAOS—This is the stage that has to do with living from a place of Faith as opposed to Fear. The main feeling during this time is ANXIETY. The definition of anxiety is fear of the unknown. Faith and an ability to manage anxiety in a healthy way are what keep us from relapsing back to the old status quo.

A. The alcoholic: You can't imagine going the rest of your life without drinking. You feel scared and out of control. You cling to your old ways of being in denial, minimizing, justifying and rationalizing your drinking and behavior as a way to deal with your fear. A part of you (even if it's a small part) feels hopeful that maybe you can get your life together. You feel terrified about changing your life and you feel scared stiff about walking into that first AA meeting.

B. You can't believe your marriage is over. You vacillate between denial and the reality of the situation. The fear of the unknown is enormous at times, sometimes to the point of crying for hours at a time or feeling overwhelmed with tremendous anger; at other times you feel hopeful about a better future. You constantly worry about the children, are terrified about money, or are anxious about what your life will be like as a single woman. You can't even begin to imagine dating again or can't imagine that you will ever find someone. The anxiety about being alone may be so great that it makes you consider going back to what you know is a dysfunctional or loveless marriage. During this stage you may also begin to get glimpses of optimism in the midst of all the chaos.

4. INTEGRATION AND PRACTICE—This is the stage where you begin to consciously learn and practice the tools, new skills and behaviors that enable the change you are seeking. As you do so, this way of living becomes the norm.

A. An alcoholic who gets sober and goes into recovery learns to go to AA meetings consistently, to call their sponsor regularly, to identify and communicate feelings regularly, and to remove themselves from tempting situations. They begin to understand how important it is to spend time with other recovering alcoholics with whom they can relate. They learn and practice tools and skills necessary to stay sober and be able to manage their anxiety.

B. Your divorce provides you with the opportunity to learn or practice how to reach out to others for support, sometimes for the first time in your life. You begin to unravel the years of an identity and life that has been woven together with your spouse. You soon figure out who gets which friends. If you have shared custody of children, you learn what to do with the extra time you now have and deal with the myriad feelings that accompany this major shift, not only in your life but also within your family's dynamics. You might go to a support group with other people who are experiencing the same things you are as you go through your recovery process. You begin to feel stronger and proud of how resilient you are. You find yourself willing to take chances, perhaps even go on dates when you feel ready. You accept that you are divorced and, in some cases because you have gained a stronger self of sense as a result of all you've gone through, you might even begin to feel like writing your ex a thank-you note!

5. NEW STATUS QUO—Once these new behaviors are integrated on a regular, consistent basis, they become the new status quo.

A. As you become more solid in your recovery program, your focus goes from "not drinking" and shifts to "maintaining sobriety." It is the norm for you to behave in ways that enable yourself to stay sober. You are accepting of your alcoholism and often see your addiction as a gift that changed your life for the better. Life tends to be more balanced and manageable. Although you have challenges (as we all do) you are now able to handle them without drinking, using the tools and community of support that you now have in place. You are sober, not just not drinking, and this is the new norm/status quo.

B. Following your recovery from your divorce you have created a new life for yourself, possibly new friends, hobbies, and often a new improved body and sense of style. You might be comfortable with dating or being in a new relationship. You have been able to let go of your identity as a married person. You feel comfortable in who you are, the person you've become as a result of the divorce. You may have been able to find a way to co-parent that works. Some people are even able to let go of getting hooked emotionally if the ex- spouse behaves badly. This stage doesn't mean things are perfect, but life is much better and you consistently feel hope for an even better future. Being divorced is the norm.

The Stages of Change Are an Ongoing Process

Whether it has to do with pursuing a dream or escaping a difficult situation, you will go through the same process. Life is nothing if not a constant cycle of change. And, having a Higher Consciousness as we undergo these changes makes all the difference in our quality of life. Embracing these changes brings about a Higher Consciousness, a new ownership of Feminine Heart Energy. Successfully going through these cycles of change is what develops and strengthens our faith.

Initially when we enter into a state of chaos, we may be filled with a great deal of anxiety. Often people don't have very good tools for managing their anxiety. This is why we sometimes relapse and return to the old status quo.

It Gets Easier: Trusting the Change Process

The Change process is not dissimilar to working out with weights. When you first begin lifting weights it burns to rip the muscles, and most people feel very sore afterwards, often this is when someone's new weight lifting program stops! But if you stop because of your body's initial reaction to this new stress on it, you won't get the change you are hoping for. Remember that as you continue lifting weights over time, it will get easier and you will feel stronger.

This is an ongoing process. As you continue to lift heavier weights, or have more intense workouts, you will again experience some soreness, but because you are now stronger, in better shape and more confident in your body, it will be easier to get to the next level of strength. This analogy is how the change process works.

Going through the *state of chaos* stage is the space where (like lifting weights) our faith gets developed and strengthened. When we go through this part of the change process with the awareness that this stage is temporary and transitional, and with the understanding that anxiety is normal whenever change happens, it is easier to get through.

Then the next time our status quo shifts, we are better able to trust the change process. As life progresses and we continue to learn to embrace change, we will have built a foundation of faith that can handle any challenges that come our way. This is how we are able to see things from a new perspective.

This is spiritual evolution. And this is why many people who have never had to deal with major life catastrophes are often at a complete loss when confronted with problems, whereas someone who has been put through life's wringer might be capable of dealing with these situations with an attitude of calm and faith. When people utilize change as an opportunity to grow, they are exercising Higher Consciousness.

Lemonade

Let's continue exploring the lemons into lemonade analogy a little further. It's incredibly difficult to make lemonade without any tools. Just try making a pitcher of lemonade without a juicer, knife and cutting board. The task becomes more frustrating than fruitful. Pun intended!

In the same way, effecting positive change in our lives requires tools and resources, both internal and external. In the example of the positive transformation we've explored in this chapter, my client Elizabeth needed what I call an "emotional infrastructure." She was able to develop this as a result of her personal growth work. In cases where people do not have a strong emotional infrastructure, they need to focus first on developing this reservoir of strength before they can draw from it.

Change, Power and Your Emotional Infrastructure

Imagine moving into a home that you think is in good shape. Perhaps it looks like it just needs some paint, a few cosmetic changes and some fabulous new furniture.

Then you find out that the electrical wiring is all screwed up, the pipes corroded. Wow, what a difference in the amount of work and cost you originally thought was needed!

Welcome to the world of someone who has suffered from unresolved major or chronic emotional, sexual, physical or mental trauma. They may not have the emotional infrastructure in place needed to function as a psychologically healthy and emotionally secure adult. Like Elizabeth, they will need to deal with and heal the past trauma before they can transform into a place of living from Feminine Heart Energy rather than from trauma and pain.

Make Yourself Structurally Sound

This does not mean people who have suffered debilitating trauma do not have a store of their own Feminine Heart Energy, but the internal tools and skills necessary to mine it are often unavailable. In these instances, it is important they develop the tools and skills needed in order to be able to repair or even gut rehab their emotional infrastructure.

If this is where you are in your life right now, get help from a trained therapist, and do the work you "know" you need to do to strengthen yourself. Don't paint the house first, denying the structural problems. Fix the plumbing and wiring internally first so you're truly safe and secure. Only then will you really enjoy decorating and living in your "home."

Dennis's Story

Dennis was highly likable and personable, very intelligent, kind, creative—and clearly an alcoholic and drug addict by the time he was 16 years old. He was without a doubt the smartest sibling in his large family, but barely made it through high school because he frequently acted out and consequently was unable to function at school. College did not seem like an option.

His entire family agrees that had it not been for his chemical dependency problems, Dennis could have done whatever his heart desired. During the early part of his life, however, his only desire was to get high. As a result, Dennis was rarely able to keep even the most menial job, never mind live up to his potential.

Dennis was stunted in his emotional development, most often behaving like a kid in puberty (the age he was when he began drinking). He was rarely able to be honest, dependable or responsible. He was unable to function normally.

His decline happened rapidly. At times Dennis went missing for weeks, sometimes sleeping in parks, and within a couple of years began drinking by seven in the morning, in order to avoid experiencing withdrawal symptoms like DTs. His life was a mess.

As Dennis's illness progressed, his family felt more and more helpless and hopeless. Dennis's parents kept placing him into treatment, each time hoping this one would take. Inevitably, they would be disappointed and disheartened each time he relapsed. And once again, Dennis would be filled with feelings of shame, remorse and guilt. His family prayed that he wouldn't die out on the streets. It was a heartbreaking situation.

Then finally it happened: prayers were answered. After many unsuccessful years of trying, Dennis finally got sober.

His substance abuse had deprived Dennis of the opportunity to grow into adulthood successfully. He didn't have the emotional or physical infrastructure necessary to do so. Fortunately, this time Dennis went into a treatment center that referred him to a long-term aftercare program, a sober living house with other chemically dependent men. The average length of stay there was seven months to a year.

This length and type of program helped him learn and practice the basics of taking care of himself. He was required to get a job, expected to be back on time for dinner after work, keep his room clean, help with "house" chores, attend all prescribed therapy and AA meetings, pay rent, and stay sober. During his therapy there, Dennis started acquiring the tools and skills necessary to deal with his feelings rather than use drinking as a way to cope.

Although it was very challenging at times to follow through on all of these requirements, Dennis managed to do so. His family and friends saw a difference in him right from the get-go. And as hard as it was to face his feelings, especially his shame, he courageously did so. Dennis got an AA sponsor, went to regular AA meetings, and developed a great support system, all of which helped him learn how to manage the feelings he had been self-medicating for many years. Dennis began to find out what it meant to be emotionally healthy. He began to build a healthy emotional infrastructure.

Dennis's maturation became further obvious as he behaved more like an adult. He consistently demonstrated more honesty, responsibility and dependability. As a result of these changes, he learned how to trust himself and as he did so, began to earn the trust of the people in his life.

Dennis has now been sober for over 20 years. His life is unrecognizable from what it once looked like. He is a role model to other members of Alcoholics Anonymous, especially the newcomers. He has two beautiful children and a wife, and he is a wonderful father and terrific husband. He is a successful businessman and highly regarded in his community. He is a man of integrity and one of the most generous and reliable people you could ever meet.

This has been his norm now for many years. Dennis's infrastructure is solid because of all the work he's done on himself and continues to do as needed. He has developed a strong emotional and spiritual foundation that has enabled him to know how to deal with life's challenges in healthy ways. Dennis has become the man he always wanted to be.

Enjoy Living Inside Yourself

We can redecorate over and over again, but if the infrastructure is a mess, there will never be a true sense of security; there will always be an underlying sense of danger, and (similarly to Dennis prior to getting help) it will interfere in your ability to have an authentic sense of power.

When it comes to your home, both literally and figuratively, you don't want to have illusionary power. No matter how good things may look on the outside, if the inside is wobbly it will inevitably seep out, like the inadequate plumbing pipes that one day burst and causes a flood, or the shoddy electrical wiring that causes a fire. When your house is structurally sound, you feel solid and safe and are able to fully enjoy it. We still need to do various home projects, redecorate from time to time, maybe do some spring cleaning, but it's basically done and we can enjoy living there.

This is how we feel when our emotional infrastructure is in place. We should enjoy living inside ourselves, feeling safe, knowing that we have the inner resources to handle whatever comes our way.

I suspect you have already done (or are doing) a lot of personal growth work. What you have done is strengthen your core, your sense of self—your infrastructure—and hopefully have created a good, healthy life for yourself as a result. Congratulations and enjoy the lemonade!

Reflections:

1. *How do you tend to respond to change? Are you usually able to experience it as an occasion for growth, or is it something you avoid like the plague?*
2. *How might you get help to manage your anxiety in order to better embrace change as a means to open your heart?*
3. *Does your emotional infrastructure feel sound on a consistent basis? If not, what kind of "rehab" do you need to do to feel safe internally?*
4. *What specific changes in your life have provided you with the opportunity for growth and transformation?*

SECTION 3

Utilizing

Chapter 11

Breasts, Hearts and Rockin' Souls

Since the 80s, there have been dramatic changes in our world socially, spiritually, physically and psychologically. There are millions of women and men all over the world who are in recovery from issues that, as discussed in chapter three, were never spoken about in private, never mind on national television.

These people have gone through personal transformations that have made them stronger, more whole, and authentically powerful. I believe that the personal transformation process so many people (like you!) have undergone has given them the tools and skills necessary to change the world.

When I think about all the millions of women (and men) who have survived histories of dysfunctional families, life-threatening illness, divorce, abuse, addictions, trauma, neglect and injustice, I wonder what would happen if they were to see themselves in a new light? What if they saw themselves as powerful ambassadors of change? What if they began to see that whatever challenges they have faced—and the growth they have experienced—were not only for themselves personally, but part of a rite of passage to become the healers and leaders of our planet?

Well actually, we can already get a glimpse of what this looks like. We can see it most recently for women in the fight against breast cancer, and the oppressed and abused women in some countries in the Middle East and Africa. Out of these tragedies have emerged movements and powerful leaders.

Empowerment, Loving-Kindness and Sisterhood

Breast cancer has become an epidemic, and as such, has been the impetus for creating a women-led movement that has grown to huge proportions. Women who have been ill and their families and friends have used this challenge to help themselves and others by coming together and raising enormous amounts of money for research for a cure, as well as providing practical and emotional help and support to one another. There has been an incredibly powerful coming together of "sisters" through annual walks, races and other events all over the country, the likes of which we've never seen before.

Women have been galvanized to confront our government officials about the need to create legislation that targets tax dollar spending to help save lives.

Breast cancer is an awful disease. It has devastated many women and their families. But as we can see, many of these brave souls have used the disease to stand up and be counted like never before. The empowerment I have witnessed in this movement has had great political, social and personal ramifications. This movement has sparked huge advancements in women's healthcare; it is a clear example of using challenge as opportunity for change on a collective national level.

The utilization of Feminine Heart Energy is obviously at work here. Women who were once victims of this horrific disease have helped one another to grow into survivors and thrivers. To battle this illness, women joined together as strangers, to nurture, support and love one another. Women have come together as family and with each other's families to assist in both living and in dying. Women have gathered together as soul sisters on a path of loving-kindness, with strength and courage, humor and wisdom. To put it in the language of our young people: Women Rock!

Pink and Red Ribbons

For several years now, women's heart disease has also become an issue on the forefront of healthcare. February has become the designated month for acknowledging the growth of heart disease in women. Like breast cancer having its trademark pink ribbon and T-shirts, the issue of women's heart disease is hallmarked by the color red.

Heart disease has now become our nation's top killer of women. Identifying women's heart disease as a serious health issue, and giving it much needed publicity via this month-long focus, means we are now gaining information, educating and empowering ourselves about another illness that has also been devastating to the lives of women and their families. As a result, we are now able to take responsibility for our bodies more than ever before.

See Your Body Symbolically

Years ago I went to a workshop with Dr. Christiane Northrup, a renowned gynecologist and best-selling author of *Women's Bodies, Women's Wisdom*. She offered examples of what emotional issues are connected to the patient's target part of the body, target meaning the part of the body that is ill.

For example, if someone has breast cancer she might have mother issues; perhaps she has feelings of inadequacy about herself as a mother or unresolved issues with her own mother. Another example might be if someone has throat cancer, she may have a problem expressing herself.

Dr. Northrup also spoke of how spirituality is connected to illness. Her talk was incredibly affirming to me, as I had previously learned some of these concepts through my training in body-centered therapies. Here was a physician affirming the same information! When a client who is ill comes in to see me for therapy I will, at some point (when appropriate) in her treatment, invite her to look at the part of the body that is sick in a symbolic way, and then see what the body is saying about the issues connected to their illness.

For example: What does that part of the body signify, what is the function of this particular body part? An example of this is when someone has had problems with their legs or feet. We look at what it is this part of the body does: it carries them, it moves them forward. So I will invite my client to examine how they may need to move forward in their lives in some way. This may mean that they need to move on, perhaps leave a job or marriage. Or it may mean they need to move toward something like going back to school or have a child. What I have found is that looking at what is happening symbolically helps tremendously.

Personal Growth Gives Meaning to Life

If someone only looks at their illness in a one-dimensional way, it limits their ability to really see what is going on. They miss out on the growth that gives rich meaning to life. In the previous chapter, I talked about how life challenges are opportunities for transformation.

I know people get well from illness and disease without any sense of higher consciousness, that they can be "deep as a puddle" as a friend of mine says. This happens all the time. But then they miss out on experiencing the dimension of healing that is transformative, and that gives way to understanding what is most important in life. Looking deeper and symbolically at what you are going through (not only with health-related situations) provides personal growth, new perspectives and, with these, usually comes peace and love.

Hearts and Breasts Leading The Way

I can't help but think about our breasts and hearts symbolically. They are incredibly powerful symbols. I find it interesting that female breasts and hearts are at this time in history the two major targeted parts of our bodies that have been diseased, and, that a movement to heal them is assisting us in coming into our own power.

Our breasts are located front and center with our hearts. They are both representations of womanhood, love and our spirit. Breast cancer is literally an attack on the part of our body that symbolizes our femininity like no other.

Our breasts and hearts are now demanding our attention, and by getting our attention have identified and created a compelling reason for women to come together to own and utilize their power.

The hearts and breasts of women are literally leading the way for communities to connect, and have transformed how our society deals with women's health care. However, I can't help but think that more is going on here than helping and healing the female body.

The beauty of the relationships and sense of empowerment through these "heart" connections is profoundly feminine, profoundly healing, and profoundly powerful. Having this Feminine Heart Energy and power out in the world creates a way to empower individual women.

This healthcare revolution has also galvanized millions of women and their families to experience the power of community. The energy of this movement and the power that has come from fighting cancer is extraordinary.

Next Mother's Day, I challenge you to pay attention to the news and observe what it looks and feels like to see televised walks to benefit and support the research and treatment of breast cancer. Feel what it's like to see a sea of women of all ages, races and sizes coming together in pink T-shirts to provide hope and support to one another. Observe the multitudes that walk in honor of their loved ones, grandmothers, mothers, sisters and friends who have passed. How can you not feel deeply touched and inspired? This is the gift. Women innately know how to heal, using their hearts and souls to guide them.

Reflections:

1. *Whether on a small or large scale, have you ever experienced the healing power of women gathering together help one another? How was that for you?*

2. *Are you able to look at the symbolism of illness in your life? How does it make you feel to think about illness on a symbolic level?*

3. *What is it like to consider that breasts and hearts are the areas in our body that symbolize feminine power? How does that make you feel about these parts of your body?*

Chapter 12

The Evolution Revolution

Most spiritually oriented people believe there is a reason for everything, even when we are in the midst of darkness. We don't tend to believe in accidents or coincidence. This has to do with faith.

One of the first lessons people of higher consciousness learn is how to live with their past by living in the now. As people get stronger and healthier, they often talk about how the "bad" thing that occurred has led them to a life lived at a level of mental, emotional and spiritual richness.

When people have "awakenings," no matter what the impetus, they gain not only a deeper sense of the meaning in their lives, but also a stronger and often new sense of authentic power. This is how we come to believe that there are no accidents or coincidences.

We Are All Works in Progress

Recently I was at my neighborhood coffee shop. I got settled at my table and began writing. A young man came in and smiled as he sat at the table next to me, and said "hello." I was trying very hard to concentrate so I said a quick "hi" and returned to my computer.

Next thing I know I heard someone singing along with the music playing in the background. Yup, it was him. I couldn't believe I was going to have to put up with this, now of all days, as I was working on a deadline. He was loud (and not at all a good singer).

He finally stopped, thank God, as his friend joined him. They greeted each other VERY LOUDLY and continued talking at the same volume. It was obvious that these two were there to work on a school project and I was hoping that sooner than later they would shut up or at least lower their voices. Nope, they were busy catching up with each other for at least 10 minutes, 10 long, very loud minutes of me wanting to kill them.

I was at my table all organized and on a roll, or had been until I got distracted by them, and there was no other place for me to sit in this cafe.

So I very nicely asked them if they wouldn't mind lowering their voices. Well... that's when I was told by the friend that this wasn't a library and I had some nerve asking them to tone it down. Again, I was very nice and said I didn't mean to offend them, I was just asking them to understand that they had "strong and loud" voices and asked if they could be more considerate.

I was then told I should move if I didn't like it, and that they were going to talk as loud as they wanted. At this point I took a deep breath and thought about this book and what I've been writing about.

I've been writing about energy, heart energy specifically, and power. So, I decided to do something I'd done once years ago very effectively with the IRS auditor. I shut my mouth and imagined sending out light from my heart to them, especially to the decidedly obnoxious friend. Shortly thereafter they began to talk in a much quieter mode. When I left, I thanked them for being so courteous, and they both smiled and said goodbye! This small incident became big when it made me once again (yes, I, like all human beings, am a work in progress) acutely aware of the power of the type of energy we put out in the world.

Being Intentional With Our Feminine Heart Energy

This—on the surface—insignificant exchange brought to my attention a reminder of how capable we are of creating change when we consciously and intentionally utilize Feminine Heart Energy. At the start of this book, I stated that *our making a difference would happen when we saw the female parts of who we are as our strength. When we intentionally and purposefully put our Feminine Heart Energy out in the world as a new model of power, we are stronger than we can imagine.*

The old male model is the part of me that very easily could have gotten in a power struggle with these two. In fact, I initially went there in my head, (oh yeah, you should have heard my brain buzzing with resentment and smart remarks). Fortunately, I chose to shut my mouth and take a breath. That day, those two guys were my teachers, giving me the opportunity to re-experience how *intentionality is the force behind the energy we send out in the choices we make on a day-to-day basis.*

My intention about how I live my life doesn't include me behaving like a witch with a capital B. As I left the café, I felt good about myself. I was proud that I didn't get caught up in what would have been a stupid, aggravating situation of my own making in an attempt to make myself feel better by creating a false sense of power. I know I wouldn't have felt good about myself if I had said some of the thoughts I initially wanted to say. It would have been easy to whine and complain and play the victim.

Thankfully, I realized that all I could do was control how I reacted in the situation, and that I was able to create a shift in the energy. This is what I'm asking you to do. No, not shut your mouth, but be very mindful about how you choose to see and do things. *Let us be intentional and conscious about how and when we use our innate abilities, and how our behavior matches our sense of self, or not.*

Creating a Life and World You Will Love

Here is another example of living intentionally, and the benefits it reaps. Sonia is a talented social worker with a very successful career. She has two terrific grown sons and is one of the best moms I've ever known. She is married to a wonderful man. They have one of those relationships that work so well you just couldn't imagine either of them with anyone else.

Does this sound like it's too good to be true? Well it's not. Sonia's adult life was created by a consistent series of very intentional choices she made about how she wanted to live.

Sonia grew up in a dysfunctional alcoholic family. There was a period of time they lived on welfare to get by. She always knew she wanted a different kind of life. She was very conscious about decisions she made, including going into therapy when she was a young woman to deal with her childhood issues. As a result, she and the man she married built a solid foundation in their relationship and purposefully created a warm, loving and stable home for their children based on the values they both shared. They had the family she had always longed for.

After Sonia's boys grew up and left home for college, she began to feel depressed and lost. Sonia knew doing a good job as a parent meant her children would leave home to create their own lives, but that didn't stop the grief she felt. She was in enormous pain about this time of her life being over. It was hard for her to see that there could ever be anything better ahead; she felt her time for a rich fulfilling life had passed, and nothing would fill the void she was feeling.

She was unable to find a "hobby" that provided her with fulfillment or satisfaction. She kept looking for something that would feed her emotionally and while looking for volunteer work, found something that did meet her needs. This was because she found a situation that was a great fit for who she is.

Sonia has found a way to transfer her nurturing Feminine Heart Energy into a new endeavor. She is volunteering at an amazing sports program for inner city girls, which integrates athletics and self care.

The mission of this program is to empower young girls through sports programs and, more importantly, leadership, nutrition and communication skill programs. The athletic piece of the program gets the girls through the door; the leadership and other programs further influence their sense of well-being and empowerment. Sonia has seen first-hand the program's tremendous impact on these young girls' lives. The energy of the program feels right for her and gives her a place to use her natural talents and interests.

Sonia's role there is supervising the social work interns who work directly with the girls. This experience is a great fit for her. Throughout her career she has often enjoyed being a supervisor and mentor to younger and less-experienced therapists. It is also a terrific match because Sonia is very athletic and has always loved sports!

Volunteering has provided her with a means to share her natural gifts, and she provides the program with much-needed help. Sonia has found a way to express her heart in an enriching and meaningful manner. This is example of someone living life very purposefully and utilizing her deep gladness to meet the world's deepest needs.

Feminine Heart Energy: An Idea Whose Time Has Come

I've talked about the change process and transformation and how it is our responsibility to own our power from a place of higher consciousness. Now it's time to look at purposefully utilizing this new type of power.

When we are deliberate and committed to utilizing our Feminine Heart Energy in conjunction with the experience and resources we women have amassed over the last 40 years, we will together create the infrastructure needed to change the world.

Every single one of us needs to think big when it comes to setting our individual intentions for the changes we long for in our own little worlds. It's as simple as that.

I just finished reading *Steve Jobs* by Walter Isaacson. Jobs was a guy who dropped out of college to begin to build his vision. In the book, Jobs spoke to the Isaacson about his drive to change the world.

He told a story about how for several years he actively and persistently pursued John Sculley, the CEO of Pepsi, to come work for him. When Sculley kept rejecting Jobs' offer for his current secure stable position—a position he liked—Jobs asked him if he wanted to spend his life selling colored sugar water or come to Apple to help change the world. What could he say? John Sculley left Pepsi and joined Apple.

Let us, too, leave behind the comfort of our status quo in order to help change the world.

No matter how difficult of a man he could be, Steve Jobs helped change the world in extraordinary ways. He did this in large part because of his clarity of vision, determination, intentionality and purpose, combined with his gifts. The technological revolution is an example of possibility and impactful change. The growth of technology demonstrates the ongoing evolution of an idea whose time has come.

Creating a new, evolved generation of authentic power by using our Feminine Heart Energy as a way to own power is also an idea whose time has come! We are ready to create a new era of hope, abundance, health and peace. Let's be very intentional, enthusiastic, motivated, determined and purposeful in doing so.

The Times They Are a Changin'

You would have to be off the grid to be unaware of how quickly technology has advanced and continues to do so. The development of technology is very intentional and its continuing evolution is highly anticipated by society. In all areas of our lives, old technology for managing the complex issues and problems that face our world is obviously about as effective as using dial-up to connect your computer to the Internet. Today, dial-up is as obsolete as dinosaurs, and continuing to utilize it would greatly impede our ability to function in our world in any kind of successful way.

Likewise, it is also imperative at this point in time to upgrade and activate our own internal technology to make the advancements necessary to better the world. We women are hard-wired with this internal technology; it is our heart wisdom, and this is why we are the solution.

Women Have the Means and Power Necessary to Lead

I know I'm a broken record. But women have come a long way; we have been evolving. We have been acquiring external resources along the way, getting some "external technical training," like the financial know-how and assets, the knowledge, education, experience, skills, and tools to access opportunities we never had before.

By utilizing our "external technical training" and intentionally harnessing it to our Feminine Heart Energy (our main internal resource), we have the means and the power necessary to lead. Similarly to our taking leadership in the cure for breast cancer movement, we are now equipped to be the instruments of change in the world.

It's critical to understand that it's not the money, sexual freedom, jobs and careers that we now have access to that provide us with true power. It's integrating the innate wisdom and consciousness we have as women with our skills and experience.

This is about integrating the outer power with our upgraded inner power. When we integrate and utilize the external "technology" we've amassed with our Feminine Heart Energy, we will be at the apex of authentic power and able to change the world. We will have created the infrastructure for this transformation to occur.

Courage of The Heart: Using Protest, Prayer and Song

The following is a wonderful and inspiring account of women who have the courage and wisdom to utilize their natural female gifts as a means to access power. The women from this third world country were able to courageously facilitate amazing shifts in their nation. They are presently working to create a literal infrastructure in their land. This story also lends itself to identifying how these women impacted one another and their communities beyond their own worlds.

My client Loni, her husband and three children took a trip this past summer to war-torn Liberia. They went on a study tour with a humanitarian service organization. It was an extraordinary experience for all of them.

What was most impressive to them were the Liberian women. Loni and her family observed a movement by brave Liberian women who stood up to the oppressive leader Charles Taylor and his army of child soldiers, using protest, prayer and song to insist on an end to the civil war.

Loni wrote an article for her community back home, sharing how these women's peace movement was credited with hastening the exile of a brutal leader and moving the peace talks forward to stop the civil war that ravaged their country.

Imagine that, women taking charge by using protest, prayer and song! The feminine spirit took over and won!

Liberia now has a female president, Ellen Johnon Sirleaf, and both she and the primary leader of the peace movement, Leymah Gbowee, were awarded the Nobel Peace Prize.

So how did this extraordinary opportunity and learning experience affect Loni and what has she done to make meaning of it in her life, here in a comfortable middle class suburb of Chicago?

She came back home and decided to do some important volunteer work in her own community. Loni is now working in a coffee shop in her town that caters to homeless teens. It provides community and resources for these kids. People who go there know that this cafe is a safe haven for homeless children and that by supporting the coffee shop, they are helping young people in need.

The volunteers there, like Loni, help the kids with their homework, finding resources like medical attention, and provide them a safe oasis for hanging out. It is a unique concept born by a woman who wanted to do something for her community, and she has found adults like Loni to help make it a viable business that can support her vision.

These women are most likely not going to receive a Nobel Peace Prize, but they can feel a sense of peace and confidence that they are utilizing their feminine heart wisdom and energy to contribute in a significant and important way to their community.

For Generations to Come

Similar to the birth and advancement of technology, we heart-centered people will be creating something incredible for generations to come. We, like Steve Jobs, the women of Liberia, and Loni, are truly capable of making a great impact. We can—and will—make an amazing contribution by upgrading the "man's world" model of power to something new and improved! Our advancement and growth as women will be a parallel process to the amazing and life-changing evolution of the technological revolution.

Let us, too, be purposeful, with imagination, creativity, ingenuity and genius! Let us, too, create revolutions that are an evolution of higher consciousness about who we are, and start making full use of our authentic power.

Reflections:

1. *When in your life have you had "teachers" who have challenged you to look at situations from a place of higher consciousness? Are you able to consistently see things from this new perspective?*

2. Is it easy or difficult for you to believe there are no coincidences and that things happen in our lives for a reason? Does it make sense to you that those who've been on a personal growth journey are here on this planet right now for a reason?

3. Do you live your life with intentionality? How so? What does that look like for you? If not, what would it take to "wake up?" How does living with or without intention relate to the values you hold?

4. Are you ready to help change the world? What do you think it would be like if you saw yourself as an ambassador of change as a result of your higher consciousness?

5. Are you willing to consciously and with purpose integrate your Feminine Heart Energy with your skills and experience? Imagine that with this evolved type of power you can contribute to advancing the evolution of humankind. How would it feel to know that doing this with intention, enthusiasm and purpose can help facilitate changing the world?

6. What was it like to read about the women of Liberia?

Chapter 13

Being the Change

There is a reason our society has had to deal with so many challenges like addiction, abuse, illness, divorce and emotional distress. I believe that reason is to help facilitate the global transformation needed for our world to live more healthily, consciously, respectfully, peacefully and abundantly.

What if all the individuals, families and countries that currently are (and have been) challenged in profound ways were called upon to be the agents of profound change and transformation? What if the new skills and tools that individuals have learned could help change the world? And what if all of these millions of people began to see themselves as *individual expressions* or *ambassadors* of God's love and strength, to help bring sanity, courage, serenity and wisdom to others?

What if, following the initial stages of the recovery process (of whatever challenges one has gone through, however long it takes), after they get themselves and their families on track, they began to see and feel that they are really here at this point in time to be part of a greater Divine plan?

Imagine, those of you who are in addiction recovery, what could happen if the millions of you walking this planet with your experiences, strength and hope saw yourselves as being here to assist in the recovery of our world? Why not? You have the tools and skills.

I'm not only talking about addicts, although they seem to have the largest club worldwide. I'm talking about so many others who've walked through the many challenges of life and have figured out how to make lemons into lemonade. I'm talking to those of you who have grown and changed as a result of the difficulties you've encountered in your life. Rather than continuing to stay in a victim stage of life, you have transformed yourselves. You are the ones who have gone from being victims to survivors and hopefully onward to thrivers.

You Are Part of a Higher Plan

Perhaps you've learned, after the initial pain and devastation of divorce, not only how to move on with your life without your spouse, but to be truly grateful that their unfaithfulness enabled you to escape a dead marriage and reclaim yourself in ways that continue to amaze and delight.

Perhaps you're the workaholic parent who learned that, even though it was hard, having a heart attack it gave you the impetus to spend more time with your family and frequently tell them you love them.

Perhaps you realized when you found the lump in your breast and were told you needed a radical mastectomy, that you are far stronger than you ever imagined, that you are not your body shape and size, and that you are beloved by your family and friends in ways you never before realized.

Perhaps you found that after all the pain, rage, and devastation you felt in dealing with being raped that you are now strong, healthy and courageous in ways that make you really appreciate yourself, that you have an amazing spirit, can now trust yourself intuitively, and that you are incredibly capable of handling life's challenges, and have a strong sense that there is always hope no matter what.

Perhaps, after spending days and nights with your baby in an incubator and feeling a love and attachment you never knew was possible, you learned that you were able to be a good mother, because you loved that baby enough to let go and say goodbye, even though you felt as if your heart had literally ripped in half. You felt how she changed your life, and would always be part of you, that there is something way beyond just the physical. You know that despite the pain, she was here to teach you and heal you in many ways. She helped you make the choice to open your heart even when it meant feeling its deepest brokenness. You feel a sense of gratitude for even the short time you had together, and more sure about wanting children than you ever would have realized.

Yes, you, all of you, are the people I am calling to see yourselves as a part of the solution/revolution to help heal our world.

What if YOU began to see yourself as part of a higher plan? How might that impact how you feel about yourself? What if YOU took time daily to send your light and prayers out to the world for peace and healing? Just this one small act could be the change we've been waiting for!

We've looked at stories and situations that exemplify concepts having to do with identifying and owning one's power. Now we will focus on consciously taking our power out into the world, both as individuals and as a culture. The theme of these stories is UTILIZING our power/energy. The following stories demonstrate how ordinary people can, sometimes out of very painful and difficult circumstances, use their situations to acquire a new sense of purpose in their lives and contribute greatly to the lives of others.

Carol's Story: Higher Consciousness and Power

Carol came to see me when she was in her early 40's because of problems related to severe anxiety and depression. It was clear from the first session that she was suffering from Post-Traumatic Stress Disorder. She was obviously a very bright and hard-working person, but constantly struggled to make ends meet. In most of her relationships she appeared to be taken advantage of, and she felt powerless to change it. Carol had been raped by her father when she was a teen. Her mother, though divorced from him, placed the blame on Carol. She had reached out for counseling several times prior to coming to see me for treatment.

Carol worked harder than most anyone I've seen in over 25 years of doing therapy. She is one of the most loving people I've ever known. Carol is someone who, even in the pits of despair, always found something to hang on to, some kind of higher awareness. When her beloved home burned down, she allowed herself to grieve and then used the insurance money to construct a place she loved even more, giving thanks for the fire. No doubt, Carol is a woman of Higher Consciousness.

Since she was doing well, we ended our ongoing treatment; she would only come in from time to time for a "tune-up." Near the end of one of these "tune-ups," she mentioned in passing that she would have loved to have been a nurse. I said I thought she'd be great, and she replied, "But I'm almost 40, I'm too old to go back to school." I told her, "So what?! I don't see why you couldn't do it."

She called the college she had attended 25 years ago for her transcripts and found out what she needed to complete her undergraduate degree. She lit up at the possibility of pursuing this dream. First, she gave me all the "reasons" why she couldn't do it, and then we looked at all the reasons why she absolutely could. I watched her life force bubbling throughout her body as she unleashed a part of her soul that she'd denied for so long because she thought she "couldn't do it."

I couldn't be more delighted to tell you that Carol went on to receive her degree in nursing. She is even thinking about pursuing a masters degree at some point. She has a resume that rivals most people as a result of all the volunteer work she's done. Carol now has a job at a health care clinic and community center located in an impoverished and addiction-infested neighborhood. She is a woman of Higher Consciousness who, as a result of getting the power an education gave her, has combined her wisdom and skills. She is truly empowered.

Carol is a great example of identifying, owning and utilizing her power. She identified her power by acknowledging her innate desire and capacity to help others as a nurse. She owned her power by going back to school to get the education she needed to fulfill her dream. And today she is utilizing her power in her role as a nurse helping others to get healthy.

Fighting Fire with Respect and Authentic Power

My friend Tom is a Captain on his town's fire department. He is a recovering alcoholic and drug addict for over 20 years. He is a man of integrity who also has a big heart and would give the shirt off his back to anyone who needs it.

Earlier in his sobriety, he gave an interview to a newspaper in his home town about his history of addiction—not a pretty picture. He let the cat out of the bag by acknowledging that alcoholism and addictions existed in the fire department. The old-timers, including his bosses, didn't understand why he needed to air this "dirty laundry."

Despite this, Tom continued to be open about his recovery. As a result, he has helped many people. He's been a fine example to firefighters and others that no matter what you've done, you can in fact change for the better and live a full and productive life.

Recently I visited his home town and had a chance to meet with him over a cup of coffee. Tom talked about how grateful he was for the tools and skills he'd learned over the years. He then offhandedly shared with me a recent incident that had occurred at the firehouse.

For some reason, Tom had gotten really angry at one of his firefighters. As a result he behaved in a way that was old behavior for him. He yelled, really yelled at this guy about whatever the issue was. Afterwards he felt horrible. Not only did he feel bad about how he had treated this man, but also he could feel the tension that he had caused in the firehouse as a result.

Tom had spent his childhood in a volatile family, and knew first-hand the stress and tension it created in a household. As a recovering alcoholic with years of sobriety, he knew he needed to make amends.

Tom called all the firefighters together. He made it clear to the guy he was upset with that although he still meant what he'd said, he was sorry about the way in which he expressed it. He then apologized to the entire squad about how he'd behaved. He let everyone in that firehouse know that he was purposely talking to all of them so there wouldn't be any gossip about what happened.

Tom told them he knew he had created tension in the house, and was embarrassed about it. He told them he was sorry. He showed that he cared about his men and their feelings.

What an amazing role model Tom was for this group of men. I have worked with plenty of people who've grown up in volatile families; more often than not, they are volatile men. This type of behavior is usually learned and can go on for generations. Tom is someone who, through his recovery, has learned how to express his feelings in a healthy way.

As a result, he was able to use his power to be an example of how to be an adult man and leader. He modeled how to deal with anger in a caring, respectful and responsible manner. He modeled how to deal with making a mistake. He was a true leader that day.

As their leader, he knew he needed to use his power to set things right. This is living in "right relationship" with ourselves and others. This is what having authentic power is about. He identified, owned and used his power in this situation. How great is it that he is out in the world demonstrating how to be a heart-centered empowered man. This is what being part of a bigger picture is about.

Star Power

Angelina Jolie is another example of someone who has learned to own and utilize her power. If she showed up at a U.S. congressional hearing most of the senators and representatives wouldn't think of missing it. If you've ever spent any time watching C-SPAN, you know the hearings tend to be boring and mundane. Most of them often look like they aren't even awake.

But if you sent in Angelina Jolie to read the phone book, she'd have even the dullest government official reacting as if she'd just discovered the cure for cancer.

As offensive as this might be to some, it is the truth. And it is the truth because what we're talking about is power. Angelina Jolie is a woman who knows how to use her power.

Let's face it: Angelina Jolie knows how to use her sexuality and celebrity. She is perhaps one of the sexiest women alive. She may be a good actress, but her beauty and sexiness are huge parts of what makes her attractive, and as a result she has connections and money, and uses both to do a great deal of good throughout the world.

She is using what she's been given to be able to give back. She utilizes her potent traits; her celebrity, her caring, compassion and intelligence and she continually makes use of them helping others.

Your Unique Gifts Matter

All of us are blessed with something that makes us unique and special. It might be as simple as being able to make fabulous brownies or having a great eye for decorating. It might be our ability to make people smile or think about normal things in extraordinary ways. We might have musical, artistic, athletic, or intellectual gifts and talents. We might be a good wife or partner. We might be a good listener or caring and kindhearted friend.

We might be able to soothe a child or an animal, knit a scarf for a friend, volunteer, organize a bake sale, manage patients on a hospital floor, lead a yoga class, be a top salesperson, or run a corporation.

It really doesn't matter what it is you are good at, what matters is that you see yourself as someone who matters. Be willing to open your heart and touch someone else's heart. Don't ever underestimate the things about yourself that make you special.

We aren't all meant to be Oprah or Angelina Jolie. But, we are the millions who can be inspired, and inspire others. We are the individuals who collectively have the power. What YOU have to contribute (no matter how big or how small) is very important to the world. It's the place God calls you, so you can be of service and help meet the world's deepest needs. We owe it to ourselves, our loved ones and our global community to create lives and a world we will love. Our time has come-Our Time Is Now!

The questions throughout this book were designed to help you know yourself better and challenge you to look deeper within your heart. So now, dear readers, how can you "be the change?"

Here are some final questions for reflection:

1. *Am I living an intentional life and am I clear about what my values are? Does my behavior toward myself and others reflect these values? How so, and how not? If not, what is getting in the way? How does this relate to "being the change?"*
2. *Ask a couple of friends to tell you what they like about you, what they think makes you unique and special. Notice what it feels like to even think about doing this. Are you able to do this exercise? If so, what is it like? And if not, what are the messages you give yourself that get in the way of asking? How might you contribute to the lives of others by owning your uniqueness and specialness?*
3. *Identify what you view as your greatest strengths. Notice how these strengths assist you in dealing with your life. How might those strengths be of use to others?*

4. *What are the gifts and talents you have? Do you acknowledge and share them with others or are you "shy?" What are the messages you give yourself about owning them? Where do the messages come from?*
5. *If you were to intentionally, purposefully take your light out into the world, what would that look like and how would it feel?*

Hopefully, spending time reflecting on these questions will help you identify, own and figure out how to utilize your Feminine Heart Energy. YOU can make a world of difference by making a difference in our world.

Afterword

Thank you for reading my book. I hope you have found it inspiring, and that it motivates you to regularly and intentionally connect with your heart as you go about your life. Living intentionally is critical, not only to our personal well-being, but also the health and healing of our world.

I believe that although the world is very troubled on many levels, there is a lot of hope for us to turn it around. The people and organizations I have written about here are but a very small faction of who and what are out there doing good in our world. To me, the great majority of the good that is being done in our world comes from people like you: People who do everyday things to make the families and communities they live in a better place. People who care and want to make a difference.

I think women in particular don't give themselves credit for what we bring to the table. We need to acknowledge that we have the power to change things, or we won't be able to make the changes necessary at this time and place in our history. I truly believe it is our responsibility as women to lead our families, communities and the world to a better place. I felt called to write this book as a way to contribute my understanding of the power of Feminine Heart Energy to the mix of assisting in this endeavor.

I will end with the amazing words of Marianne Williamson, a visionary and leader with heart and smarts. I keep a copy of these words with me in my appointment book and pull it out often, especially when I am feeling inadequate. It is a reminder to me that I am here to serve the world.

"Our deepest fear is not that we are inadequate. Our deepest fear is that we are powerful beyond measure. It is our light, not our darkness that most frightens us. We ask ourselves, Who am I to be brilliant, gorgeous, talented, fabulous? Actually, who are you not to be? You are a child of God. Your playing small does not serve the world. There is nothing enlightened about shrinking so that other people won't feel insecure around you. We are all meant to shine, as children do. We were born to make manifest the glory of God that is within us. It's not just in some of us; it's in everyone. And as we let our own light shine, we unconsciously give other people permission to do the same. As we are liberated from our own fear, our presence automatically liberates others."

- Marianne Williamson

May you let your light shine brightly and, may you always remember who you truly are.

Peace and blessings,
Mary Ann

About the Author

Mary Ann Daly, M.A., LCPC, is a Chicago-based psychotherapist, workshop leader and consultant who focuses on helping women find their inner voice and strength. She holds a masters degree in counseling and psychology and has over 25 years experience in private practice. Mary Ann's workshops and retreats on trauma and recovery; prosperity and spirituality; alcoholism and family issues; and women and power have helped countless women and men tap in to their Feminine Heart Energy and learn to lead more productive, meaningful and fulfilled lives.

To find out about Mary Ann's upcoming events or to contact her, go to her website @ www.madaly.com

Printed in the United States
By Bookmasters